PARENTING: YOU WILL NEVER PEE ALONE AGAIN

Therapeutic Comics For Very, Very Tired Moms and Dads

BY BRENDA LI

www.SummerandMuu.com

For permissions contact:

Brenda@SummerandMuu.com

Paperback:
ISBN-13: 978-1775217305
ISBN-10: 1775217302

Ebook:
ISBN-13: 978-1775217312
ISBN-10: 1775217310

SUMMER&MUU™
summerandmuu.com

DEDICATED TO

All my family and friends who believed in me,
laughing at everything I draw.

MY MOM AND DAD, for raising me with unconditional
love, support and good food. Thank you for giving me advice on
life, always babysitting, feeding and bathing my kid!!

MY HUSBAND, for believing in me, listening to me talk
endlessly about anything. You lead, and you guide. Thank you for
keeping me organized and for always picking up my socks.

MY SISTER, for always being there even though we are
miles apart, answering my questions on life and shedding light on
bigger perspectives. Oh, and she made me thank her cat, Mitten.

MY SON, we love you to the moon and back. You are the
inspiration of my comics. If you are well-behaved, then this book
would be boring wouldn't it? Thank you for your smiles, your
hugs, your kisses, and even your poop and tantrums. You held our
hands and taught us patience, understanding and love.

INTRODUCTION

I lost a very close girlfriend to postpartum depression. I miss her a lot. Her son was only 2 months old at the time. Like all moms, she wanted to give her son the best of everything, putting a lot of pressure on herself.

To all new moms, fed is best. Moms should be supported, and not judged, in choosing any feeding options for their babies. Whether it's breast milk, formula, or a combination of both. There is no right or wrong way. Do whatever it takes to survive. What kept me going was knowing that everything is a phase and that the difficult moments will not last forever.

Parenting is not easy and it will not be perfect. You will make mistakes day after day, but who cares? Your children won't notice - they will still think you're the best.

I hope that after this book, you would realize that you are not alone in this parenting journey and that there is no privacy in parenting. Kids grow up so fast - soon you will miss those days where they climb all over you and watch you pee.

MAMA WILL BE OUT SHORTLY! OK SWEETIE?

NO

Love and Hugs!!
Brenda

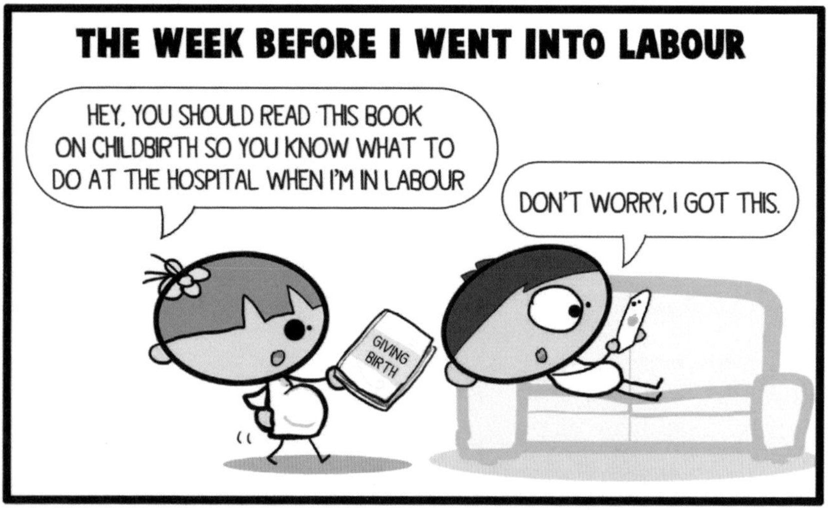
THE WEEK BEFORE I WENT INTO LABOUR
HEY, YOU SHOULD READ THIS BOOK ON CHILDBIRTH SO YOU KNOW WHAT TO DO AT THE HOSPITAL WHEN I'M IN LABOUR
DON'T WORRY, I GOT THIS.
GIVING BIRTH

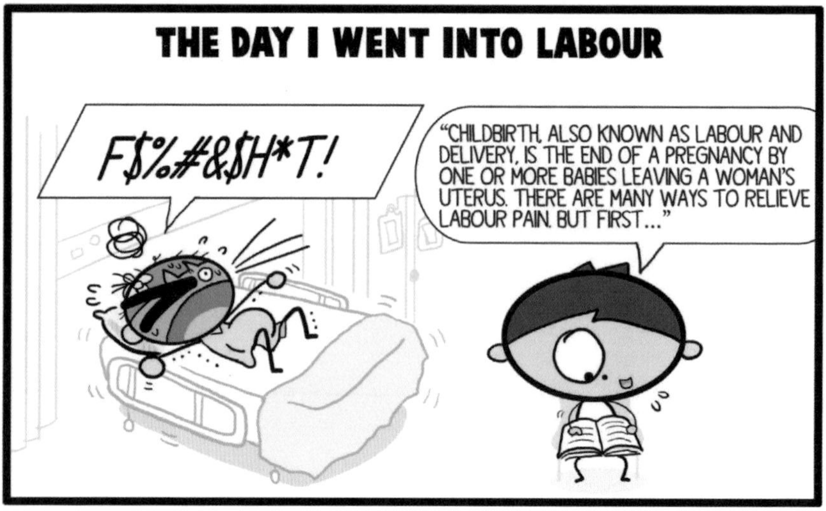
THE DAY I WENT INTO LABOUR
F$%#&$H*T!
"CHILDBIRTH, ALSO KNOWN AS LABOUR AND DELIVERY, IS THE END OF A PREGNANCY BY ONE OR MORE BABIES LEAVING A WOMAN'S UTERUS. THERE ARE MANY WAYS TO RELIEVE LABOUR PAIN. BUT FIRST..."

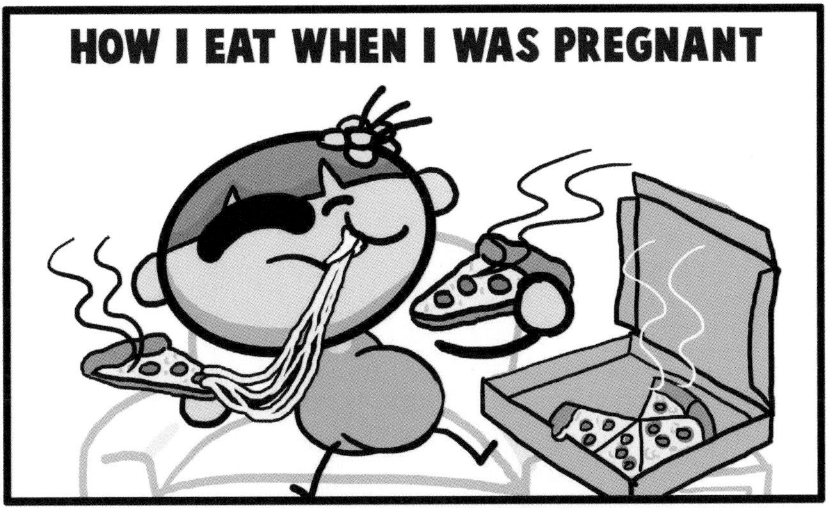
HOW I EAT WHEN I WAS PREGNANT

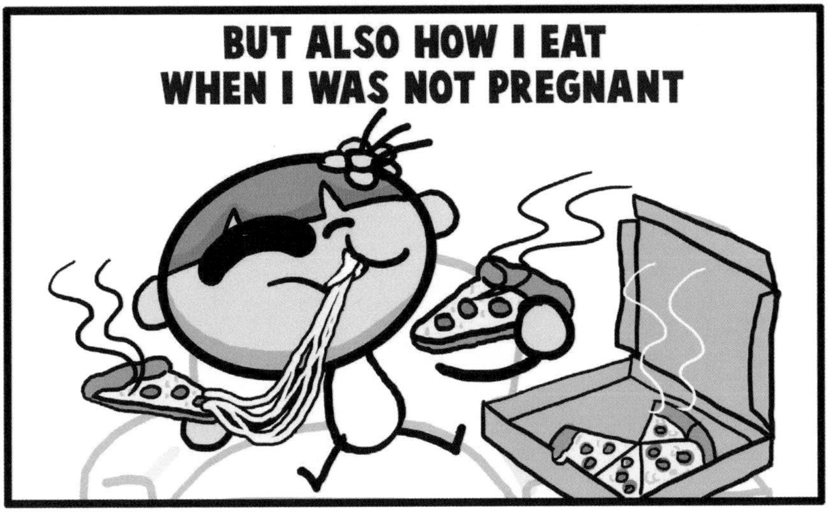
BUT ALSO HOW I EAT
WHEN I WAS NOT PREGNANT

DAILY QUESTION I HAVE TO ANSWER

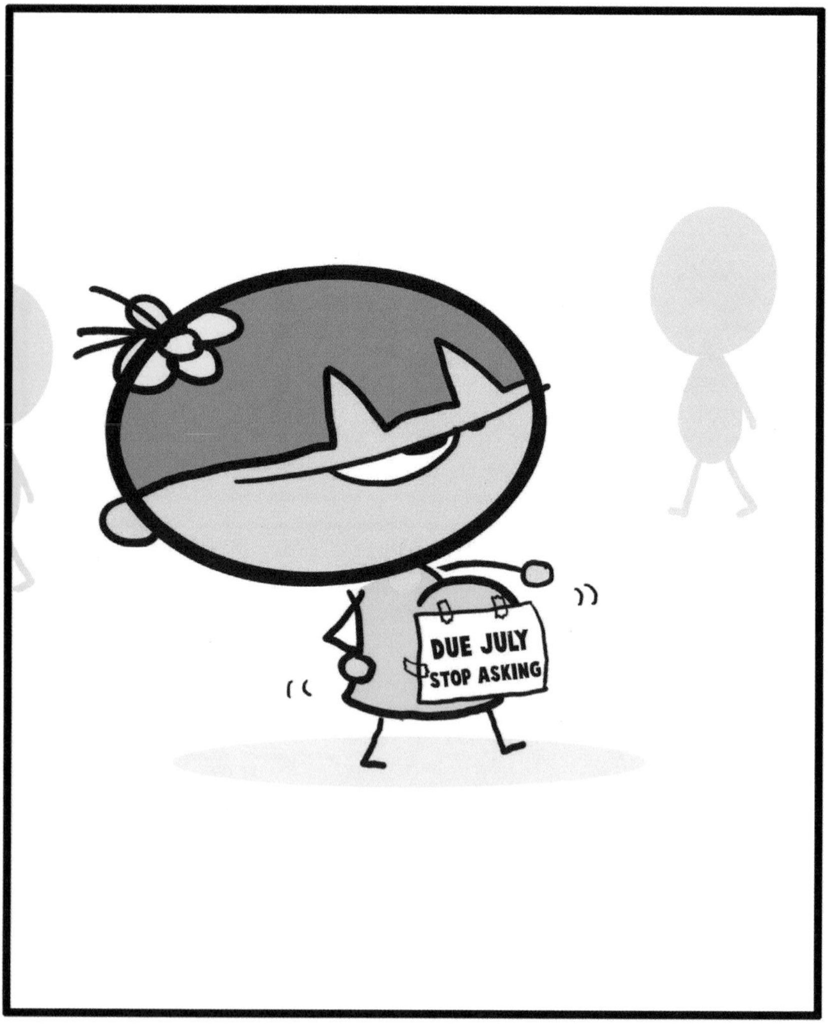
DUE JULY
STOP ASKING

HAVING A BABY

MY WIFE IS HAVING A BABY!
HERE, FILL THESE FORMS
WHICH EMAIL SHOULD I PUT...

AND HE'S OUT...

TWINKLE TWINKLE LITTLE STAR
HOW I WONDER WHAT YOU -
!
AAARH!!

NEED MORE CUSHIONS

I PLACED CUSHIONS ALL AROUND MY BABY TO PROTECT HIS HEAD WHEN HE WAS LEARNING TO SIT
SH*T.

ALL DONE!

WOW, ARE YOU ALL DONE??
OK, LET'S GET YOU OUT!
WHAT A GOOD BOY.

GIMME A KISS

COME GIVE MAMA A KISS!
BONK!
!

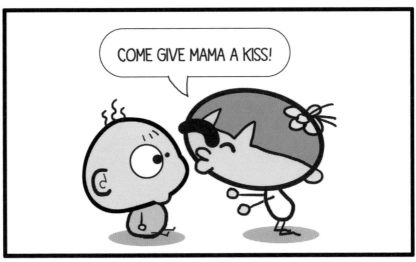

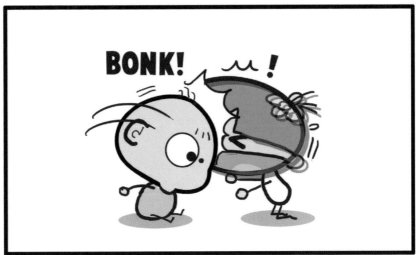

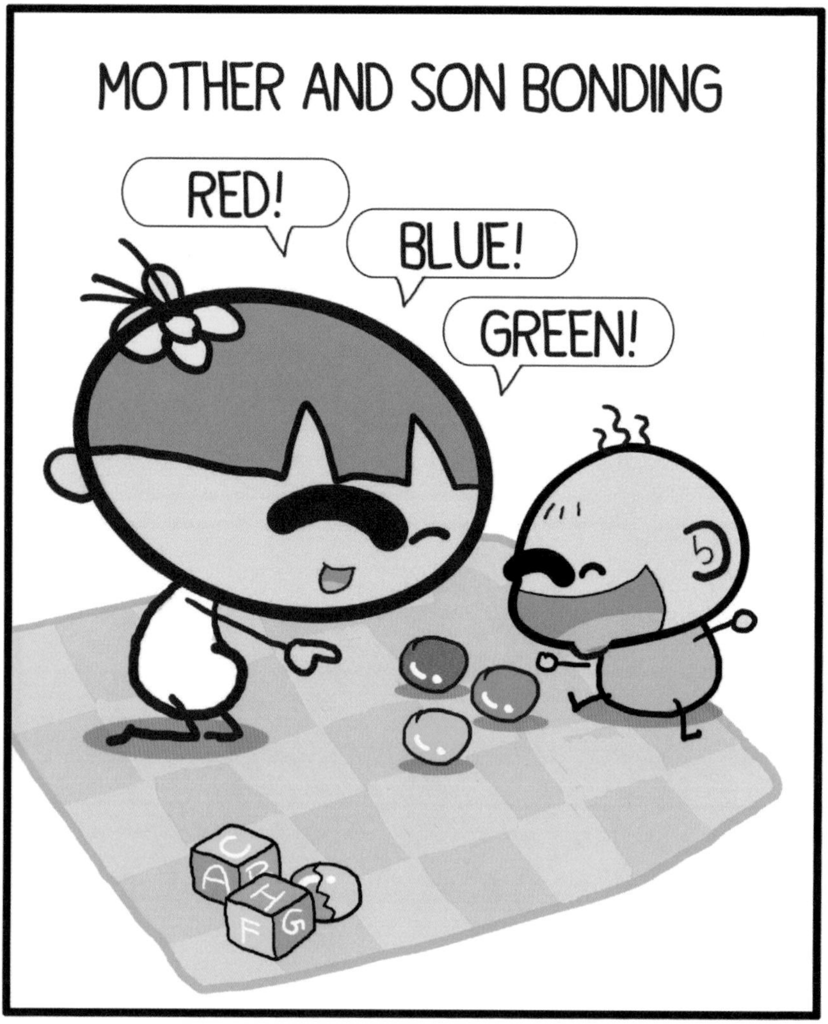
MOTHER AND SON BONDING
RED!
BLUE!
GREEN!

FATHER AND SON BONDING

THINGS I NEED TO DO
BEFORE I CAN GO OUT
AND LEAVE THE BABY
WITH MY HUSBAND

NURSE
NURSE

PUMP
PUMP

POUR
POUR

WASH
WASH

STIR
STIR

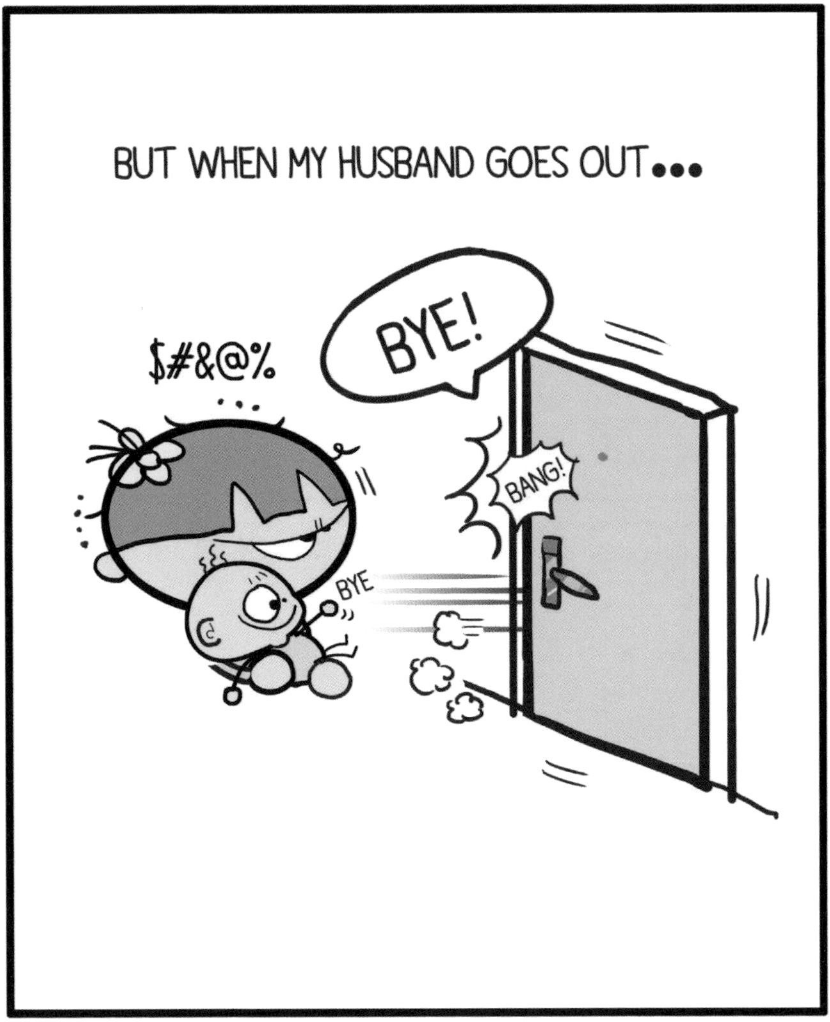
BUT WHEN MY HUSBAND GOES OUT...
BYE!
$#&@%
BANG!
BYE

MEN

MUU LIFTS A COUPLE HUNDRED POUNDS AT THE GYM
NO PROBLEM
BUT WHEN IT COMES TO CARRYING A BABY...
OH HE IS SO HEAVY

MAKE SURE YOU NEED IT BEFORE YOU BUY IT

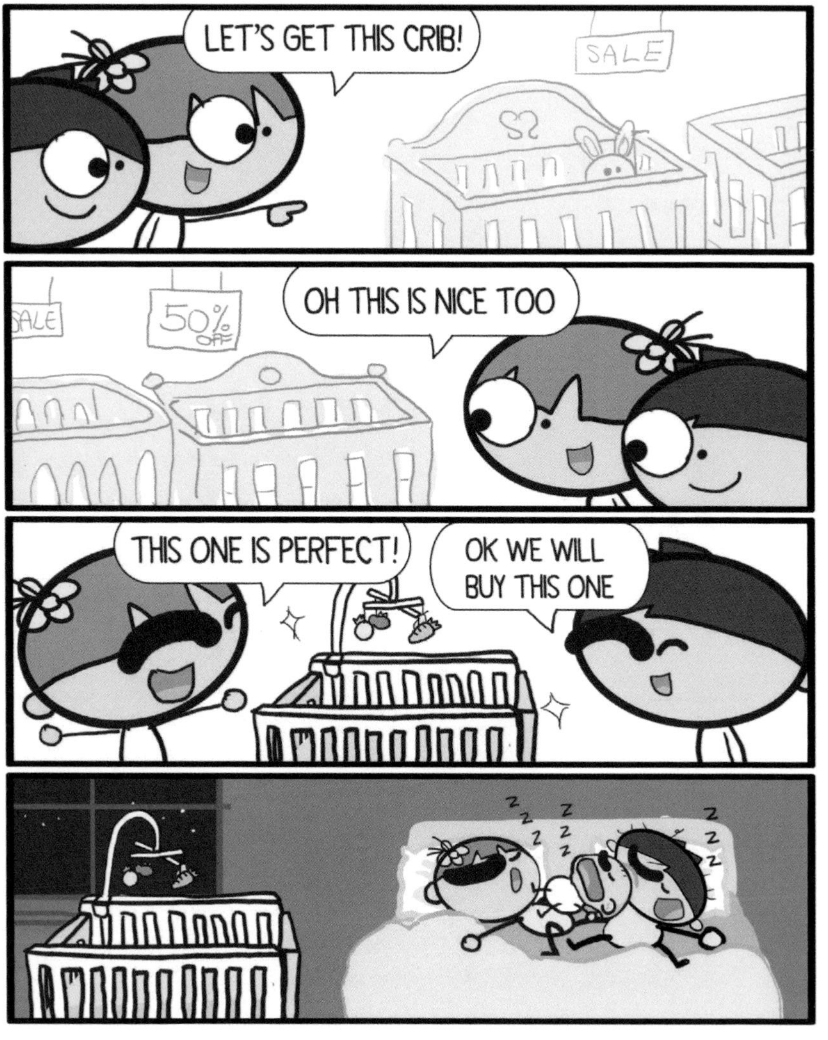

LET'S GET THIS CRIB!
SALE
SALE
50% OFF
OH THIS IS NICE TOO
THIS ONE IS PERFECT!
OK WE WILL BUY THIS ONE
Z Z Z Z Z Z Z Z Z

SPENT SO MUCH TIME CHOOSING THE PERFECT STROLLER
ADJUSTABLE CANOPY
MULTIPLE RECLINE POSITIONS
SNACK AND TOY TRAY
LARGE STORAGE BASKET
FRONT SWIVEL WHEELS
ADJUSTABLE HANDLE BAR
REMOVABLE CUP HOLDER
5-POINT SAFETY HARNESS
ONE-HAND COMPACT FOLD
COMFORTABLE FOOTREST
GET IN.....

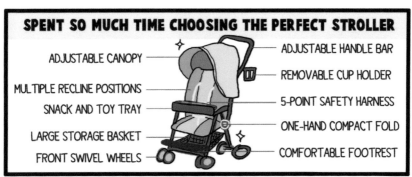

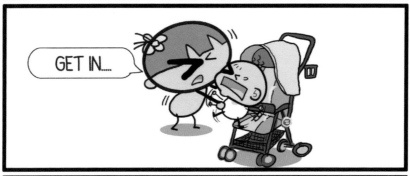

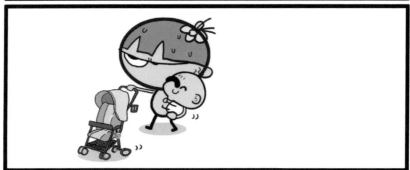

PUTTING BABY TO SLEEP

CAN YOU PUT OUR SON TO BED TONIGHT?
NO PROBLEM!
Z
Z
Z

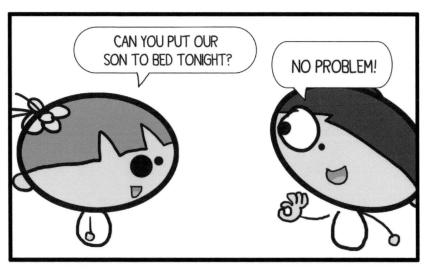

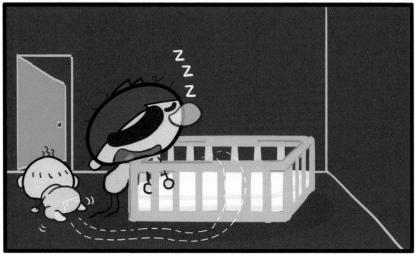

BEFORE AND AFTER

I USED TO CHASE DREAMS
NOW I CHASE NAKED BUMS

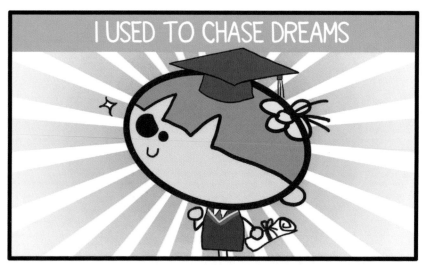

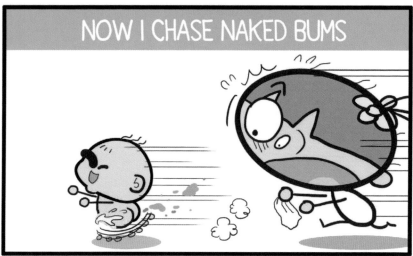

BABIES ARE SMARTER THAN WE THINK

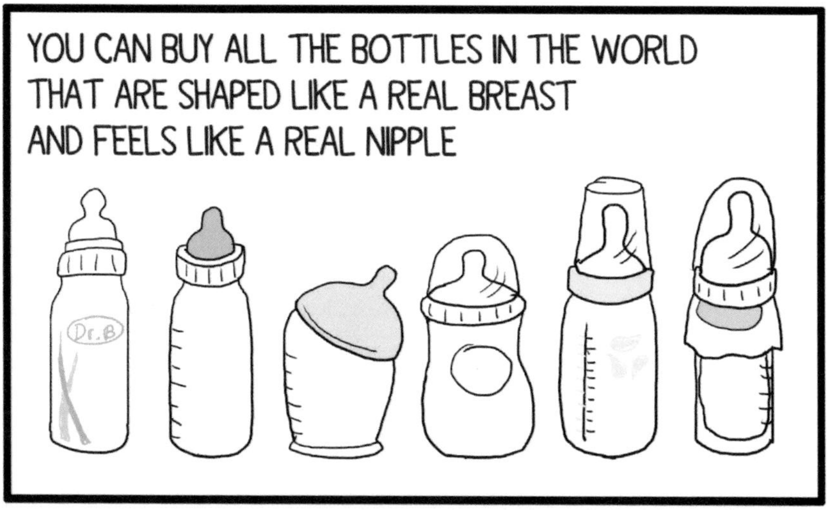
YOU CAN BUY ALL THE BOTTLES IN THE WORLD
THAT ARE SHAPED LIKE A REAL BREAST
AND FEELS LIKE A REAL NIPPLE
Dr.B

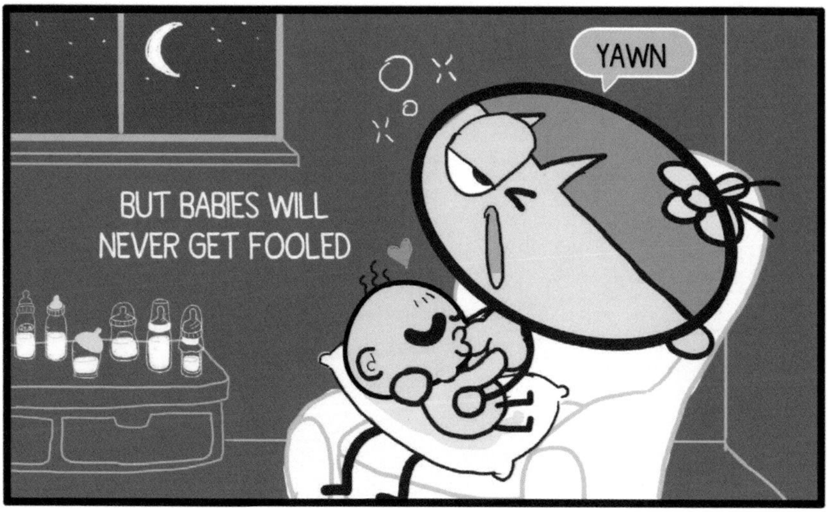
YAWN
BUT BABIES WILL
NEVER GET FOOLED

NO SCREEN TIME

YOU GO SHOWER HONEY. I GOT THIS.
MAKE SURE HE DOESN'T WATCH TV THIS TIME!
NO PROBLEM!
HERE PLAY WITH THIS, IT'S FUN.

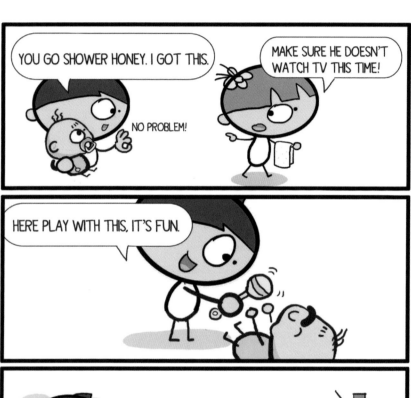

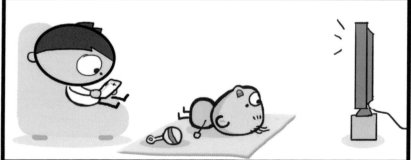

HE IS A GREAT SLEEPER

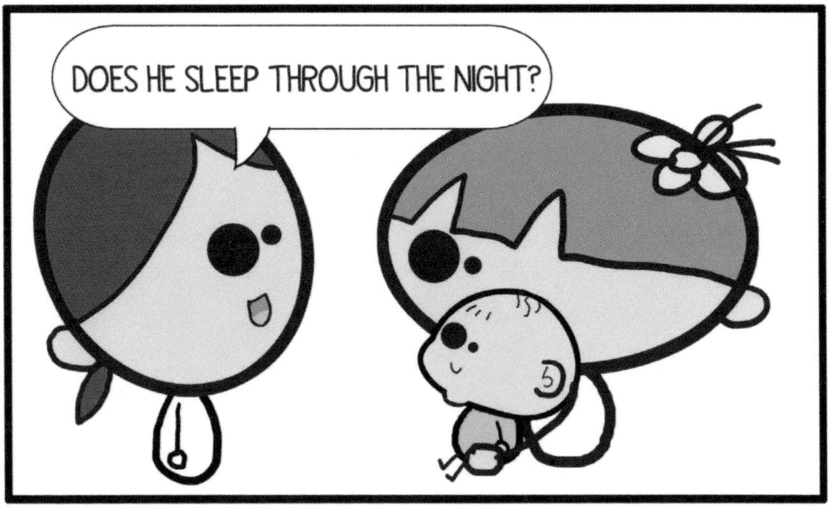
DOES HE SLEEP THROUGH THE NIGHT?

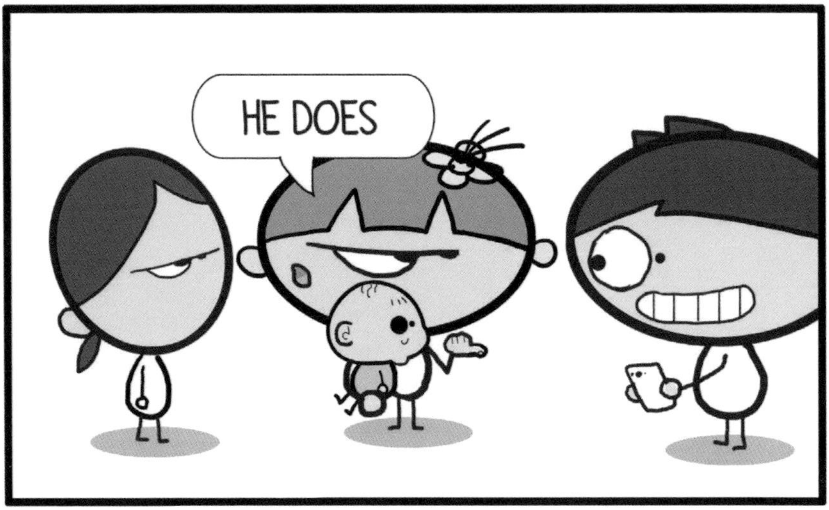
HE DOES

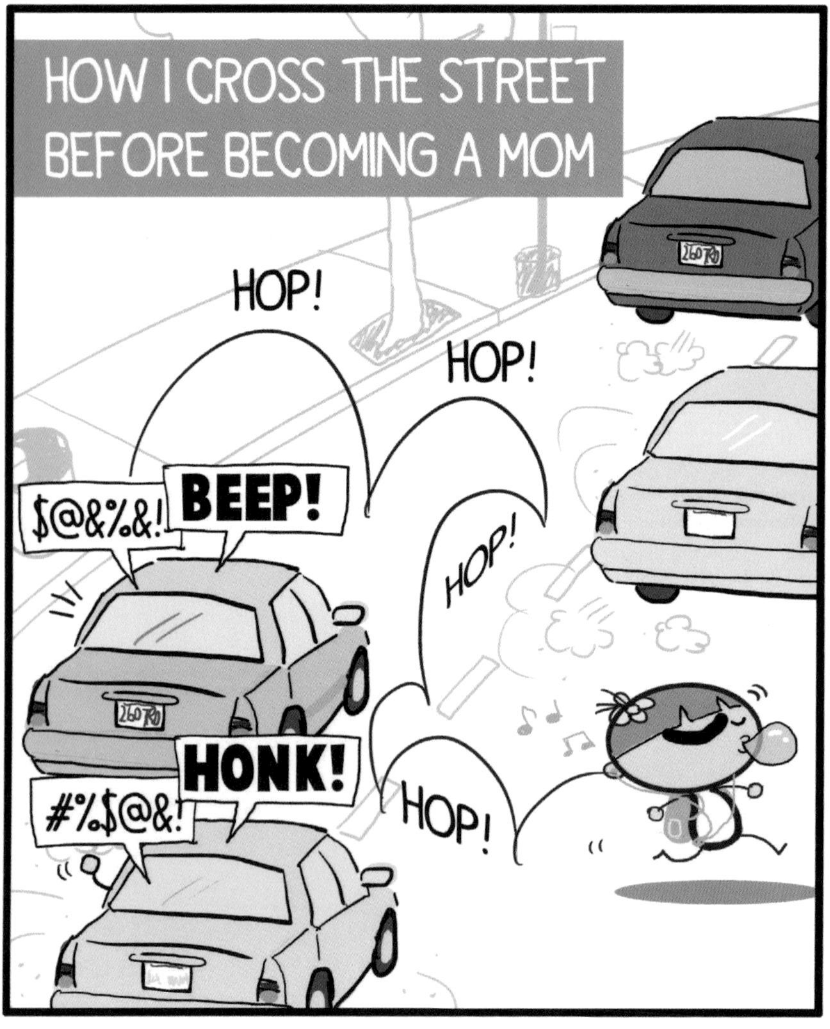
HOW I CROSS THE STREET
BEFORE BECOMING A MOM
HOP!
HOP!
HOP!
HOP!
$@&%&!
BEEP!
HONK!
#%$@&!

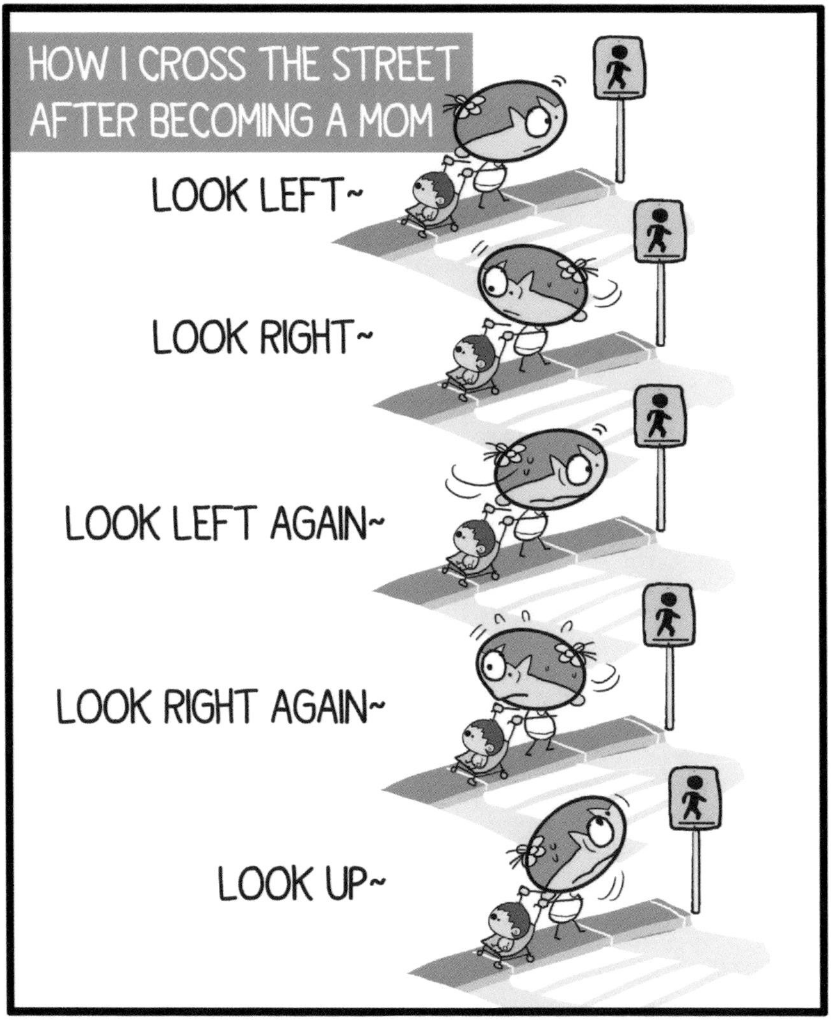
HOW I CROSS THE STREET AFTER BECOMING A MOM
LOOK LEFT~
LOOK RIGHT~
LOOK LEFT AGAIN~
LOOK RIGHT AGAIN~
LOOK UP~

WHAT BABIES LOVE MOST

TOYS
NOPE
TISSUE BOX
YES!!

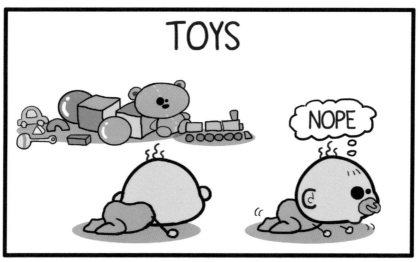

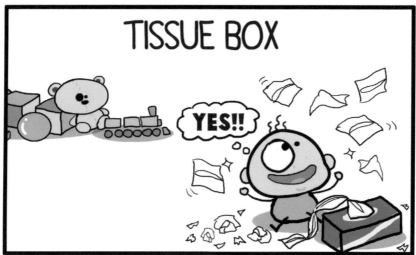

EATING WITH A BABY

IF I'M HOLDING THE BABY, I AM VERY CAREFUL WHEN I EAT
Z
Z
Z
MY HUSBAND? NOT SO MUCH.

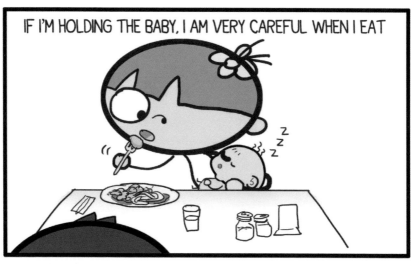

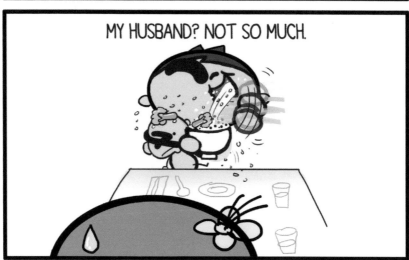

NOM NOM NOM

HERE, GET CREATIVE
NOM
NOM
NOM

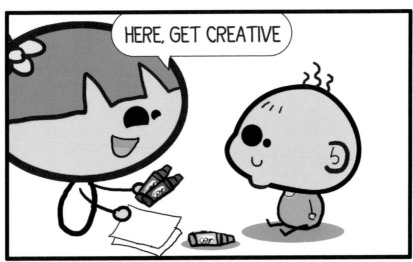

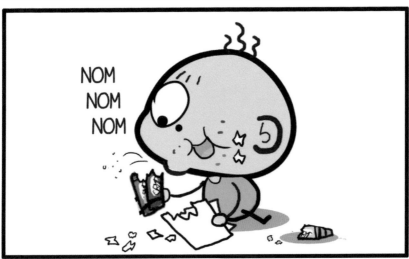

WHAT ABOUT THE RIGHT FOOT?

OH NO, DON'T EAT THAT!
GOOD BOY
DROPS
NO, YOU CAN'T EAT THE RIGHT FOOT EITHER

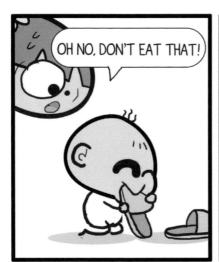

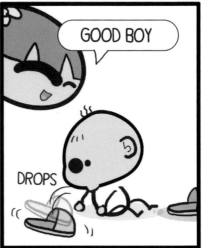

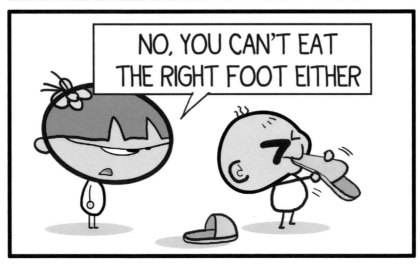

DAD KNOWS BEST

OH YOU POOR BABY!!!
WAAAA!
DON'T WORRY, MAMA'S HERE
WAAAA!
STOP PRETENDING

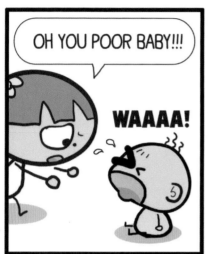

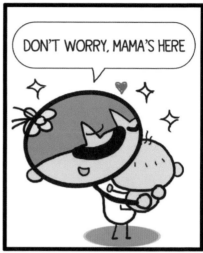

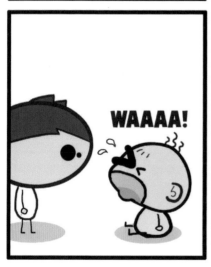

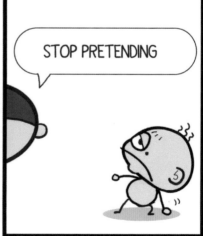

HAPPY BABY

MA!
MA!
MA!
3:00AM

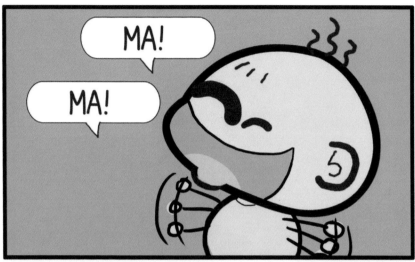

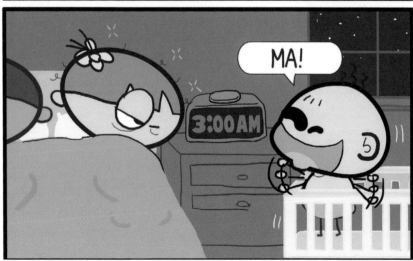

STRATEGY

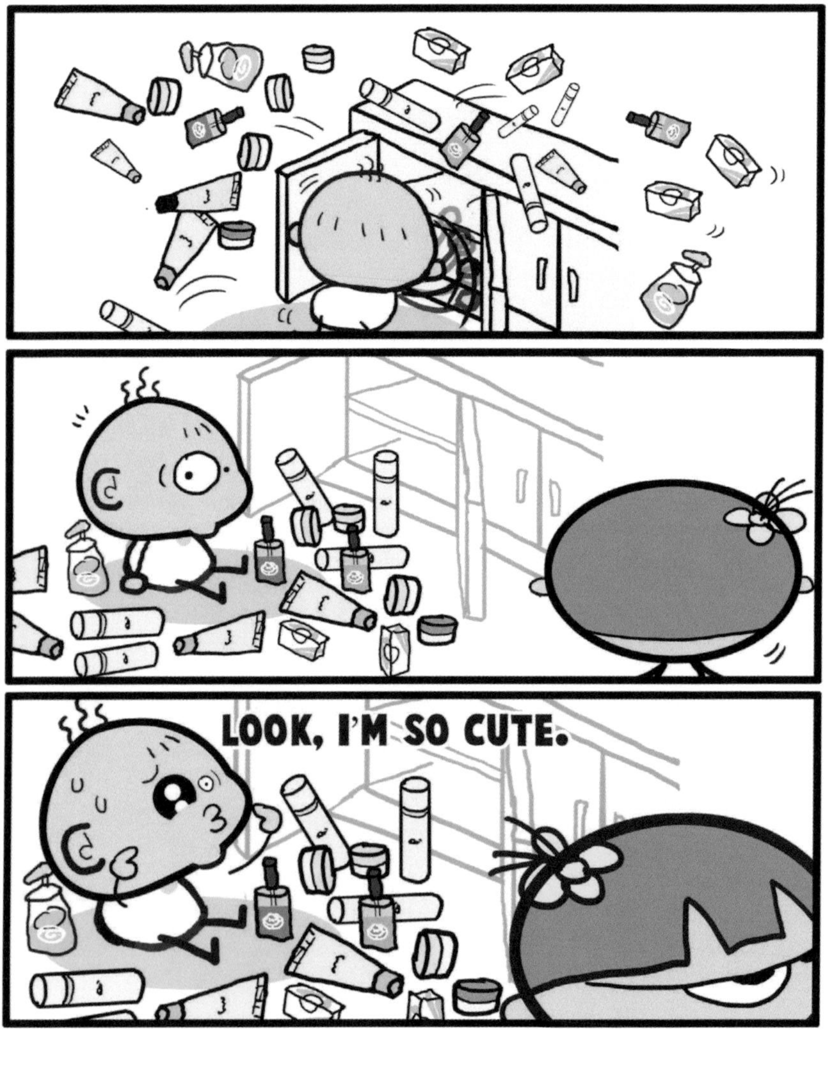
LOOK, I'M SO CUTE.

HE IS TALKING!

OMG! HE'S TALKING!!!
MY SON IS FINALLY TALKING?
NO, YOUR HUSBAND.
HE NEVER TALKS. BUT NOW LOOK!
PEEKABOO!

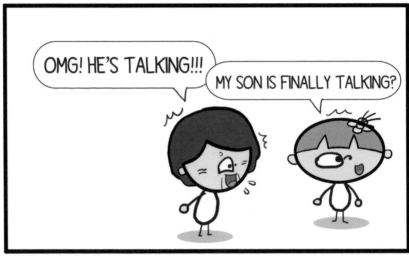

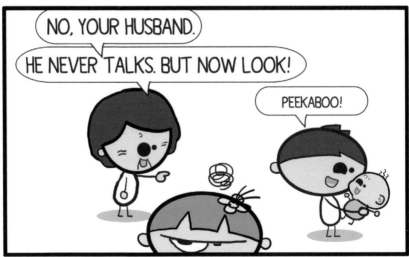

SOME THINGS REQUIRE 100% CONFIRMATION

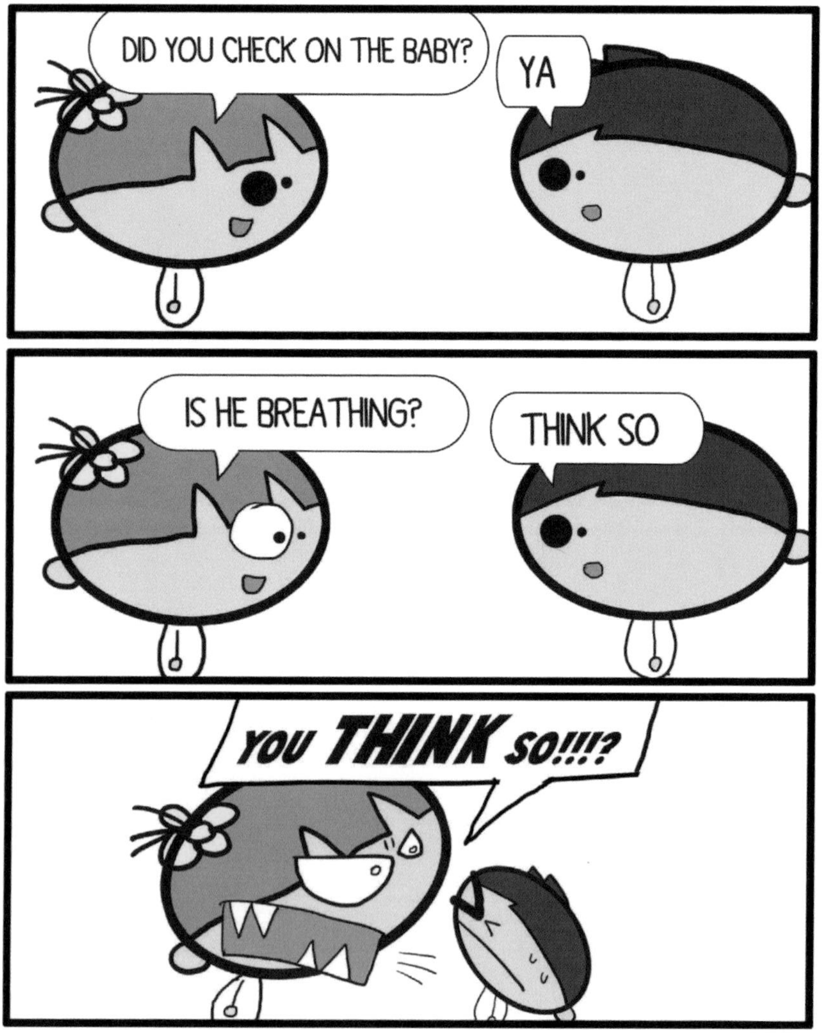
DID YOU CHECK ON THE BABY?
YA
IS HE BREATHING?
THINK SO
YOU THINK SO!!!?

ALL OF 3 SECONDS

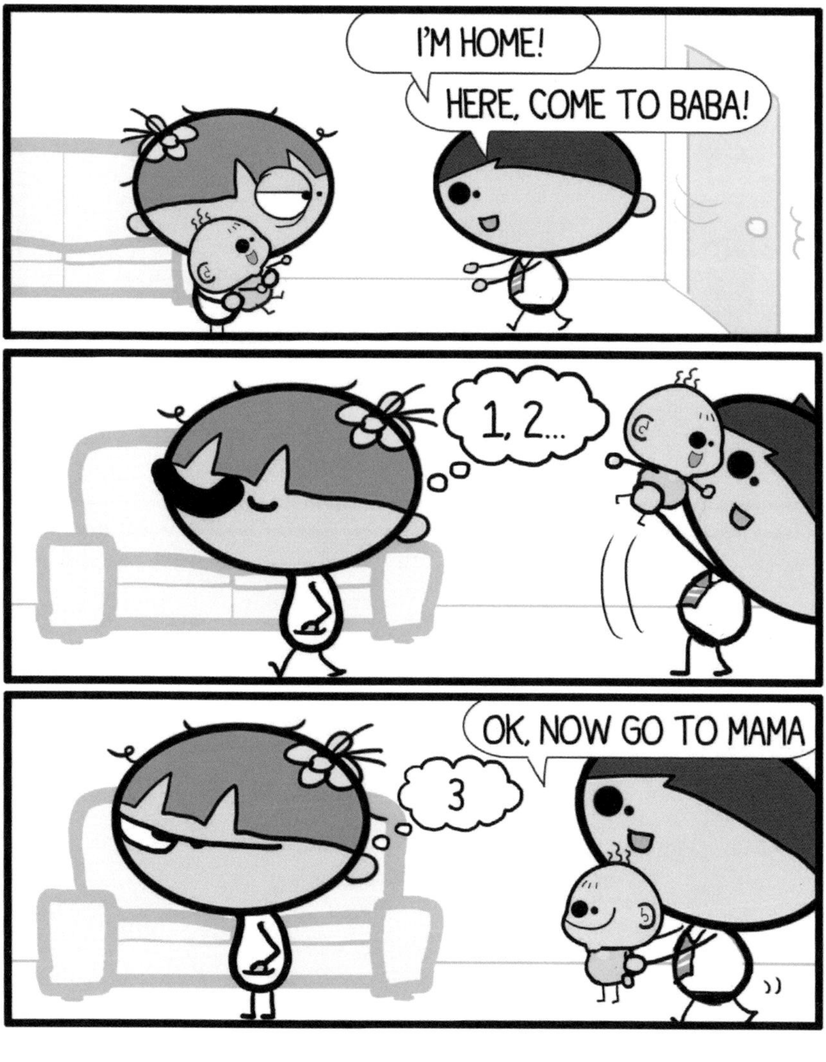

I'M HOME!
HERE, COME TO BABA!
1, 2...
OK, NOW GO TO MAMA
3

PLAYING WITH HIS SON

HERE, PLAY WITH HIM

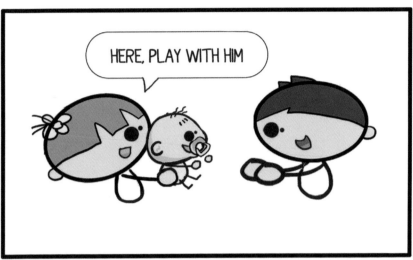

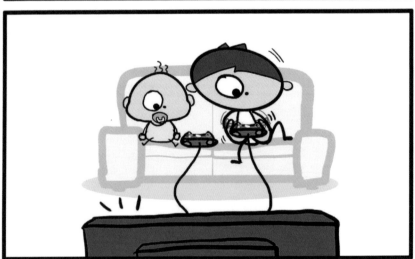

MY HUSBAND, TRYING TO BE HELPFUL

HERE, LET ME TAKE HIM. YOU GO CONCENTRATE ON YOUR COMICS.
WAAAAA!
WAA!
WAA!
WAA!
WAA!
WAA!
WAA!
WAA!
WAA!

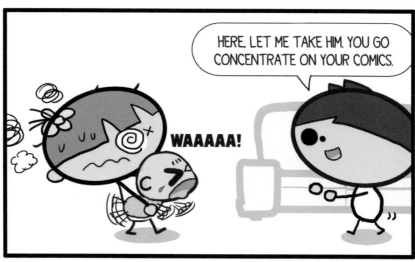

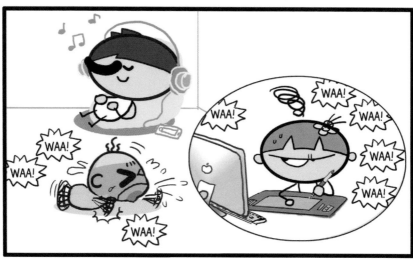

CHANGE OF PLANS

OKAY, HERE'S THE PLAN.
MY BABY WILL NOT GET SCREEN TIME UNTIL HE IS 2 YEARS OLD
WAAAA!
WAAAA!
WAAAA!
NEVERMIND

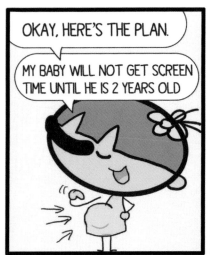

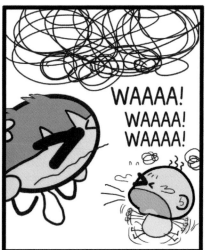

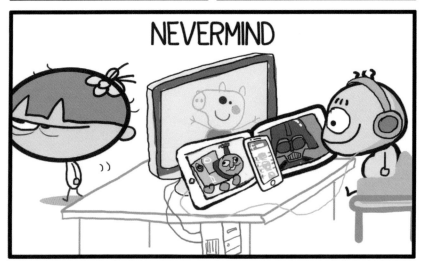

REFRESHED

WHEW! FINALLY PUT MY SON TO NAP.
Z Z Z
3 MINUTES LATER
ALL DONE!

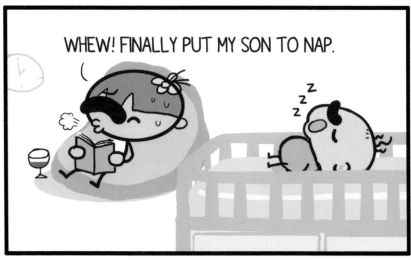

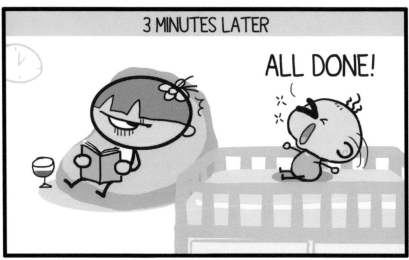

CONDITIONAL SUPPORT

MOMMY LOVES YOU.
I WILL ALWAYS SUPPORT
WHATEVER YOU DO
NO!
NO!
NOOO!

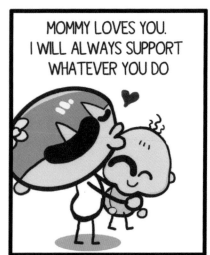

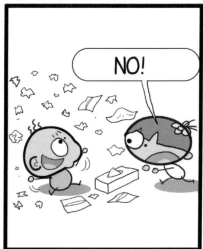

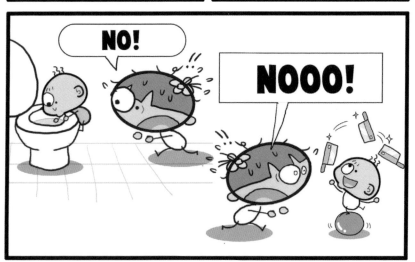

START EARLY

PREPARING MY CHILD FOR SUCCESS
TODAY, WE LEARN ABOUT ABC
B
C
A
$A^2+B^2=C^2$

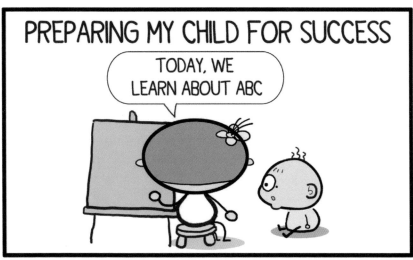

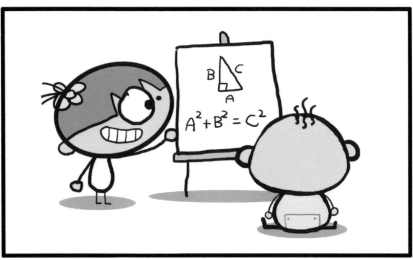

EVERY, SINGLE, TIME.

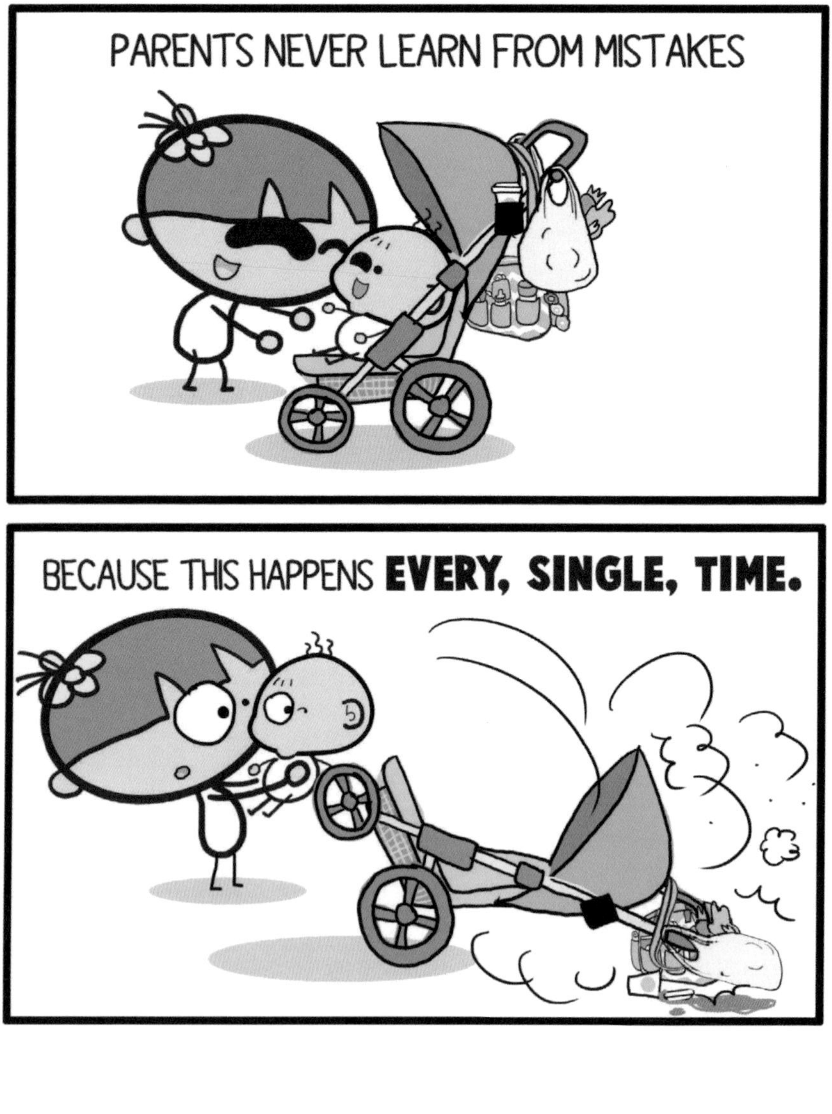
PARENTS NEVER LEARN FROM MISTAKES
BECAUSE THIS HAPPENS **EVERY, SINGLE, TIME.**

JUST SOUNDS

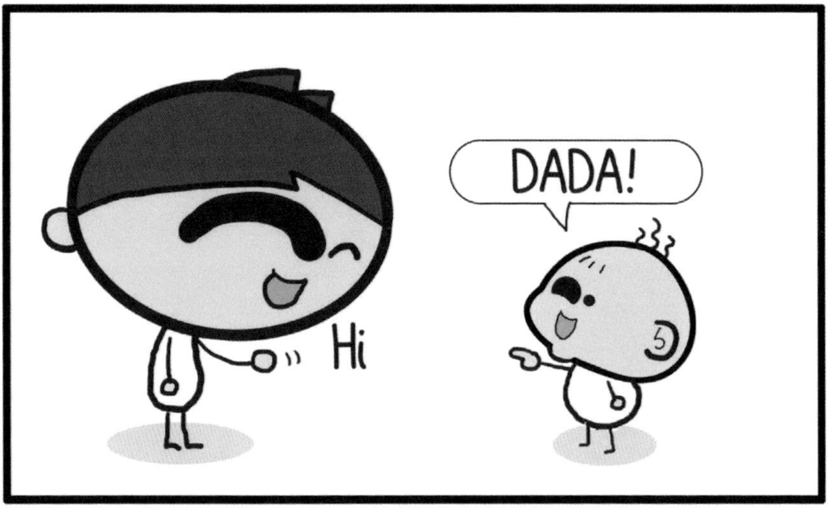
Hi
DADA!

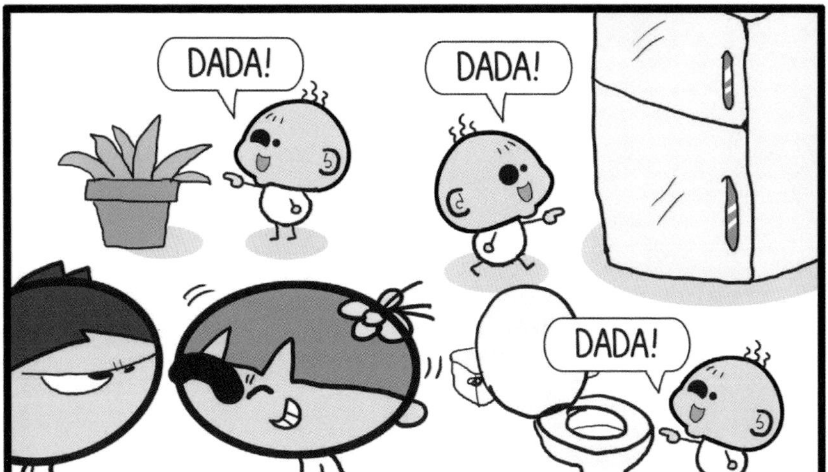
DADA!
DADA!
DADA!

SPORTS

IS OUR SON GONNA PLAY HOCKEY LIKE YOU WHEN HE GROWS UP?
NOPE, HE CAN PLAY SOCCER.

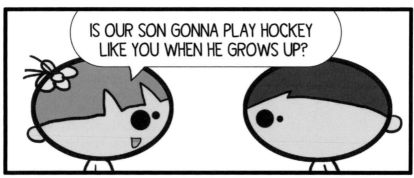

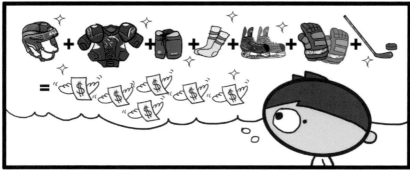

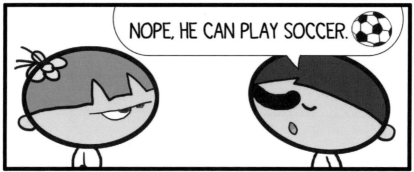

FART

SSSHHH~
Z Z Z
FART
WAAAA!

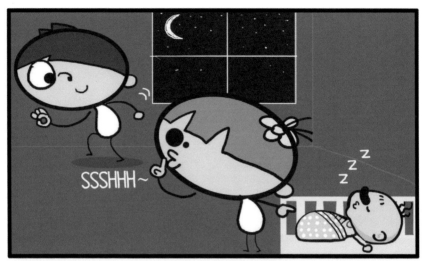

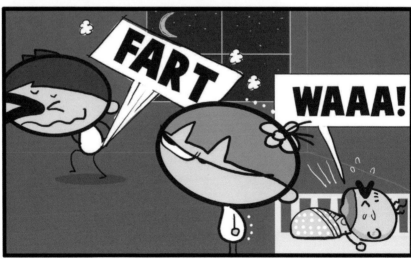

WHAT TIME IS IT

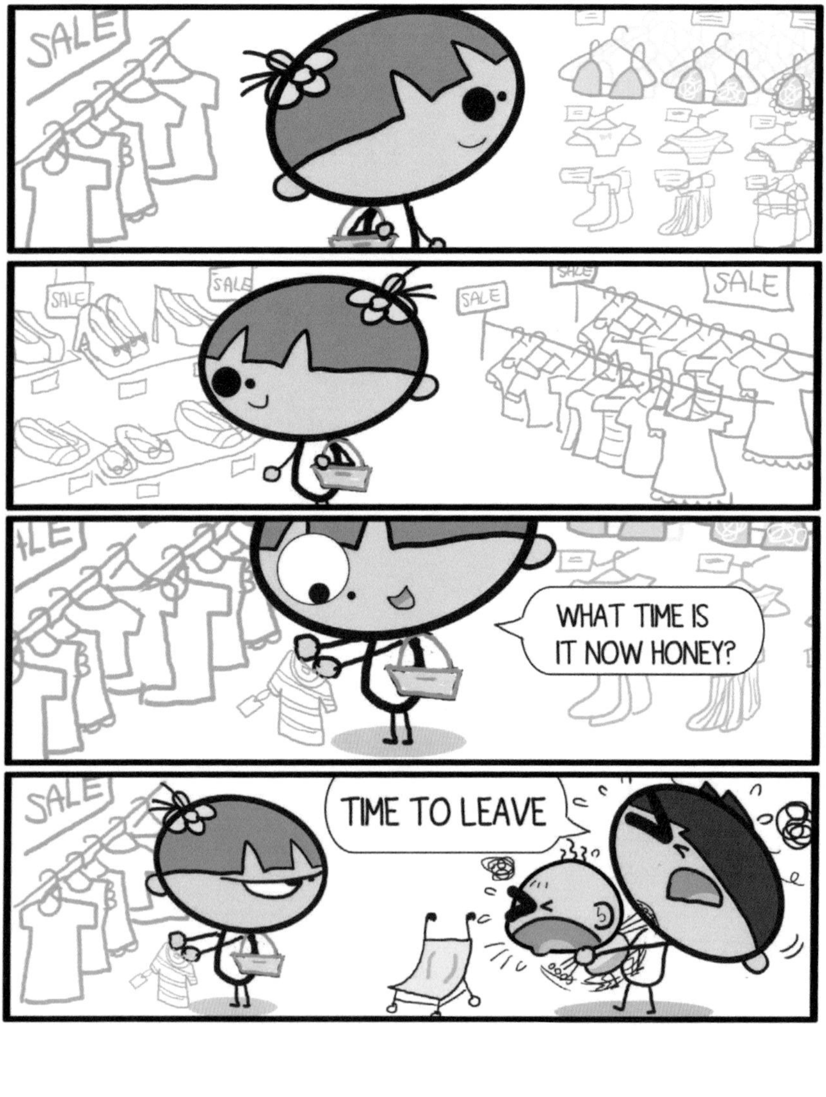
SALE
SALE
SALE
SALE
SALE
SALE
WHAT TIME IS IT NOW HONEY?
SALE
TIME TO LEAVE

THE BOTTLE

CAN YOU PASS ME THE BOTTLE ?
NO, THE OTHER BOTTLE

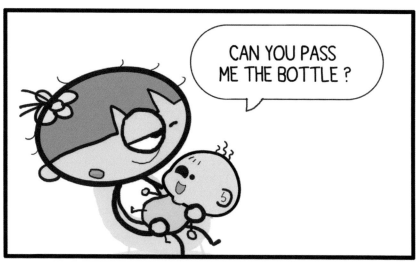

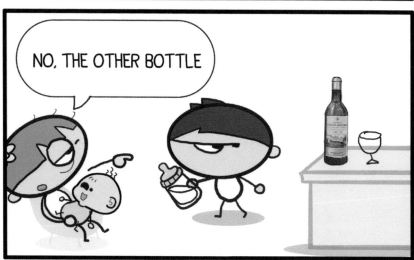

TODDLERS

DON'T LEAVE ME MAMA!

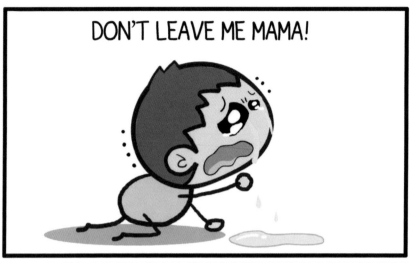

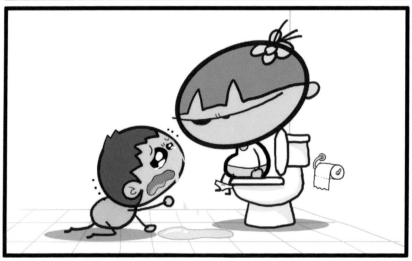

ALARM

MY ALARM BACK THEN
MY ALARM NOW
Z Z Z

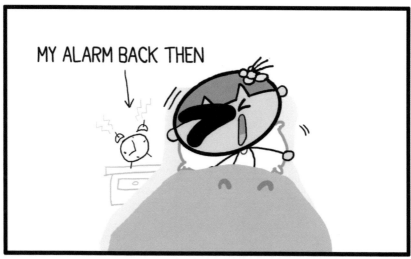

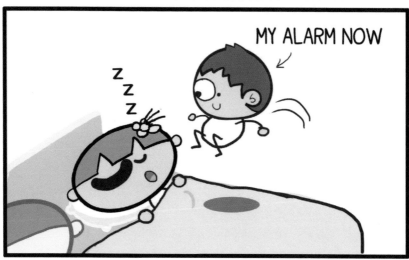

TIME TO GO HOME NOW

OK, 5 MORE MINUTES!
5 MORE MINUTES
WEEE!
5 MORE MINUTES

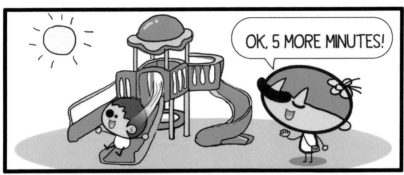

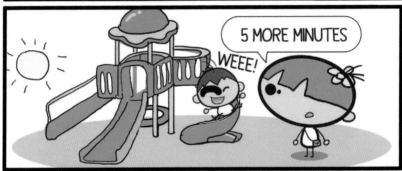

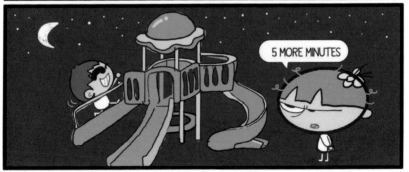

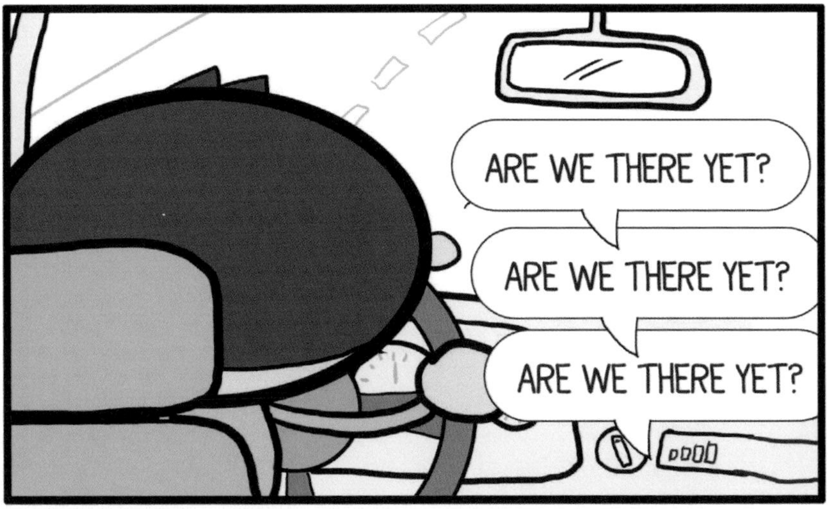
ARE WE THERE YET?
ARE WE THERE YET?
ARE WE THERE YET?

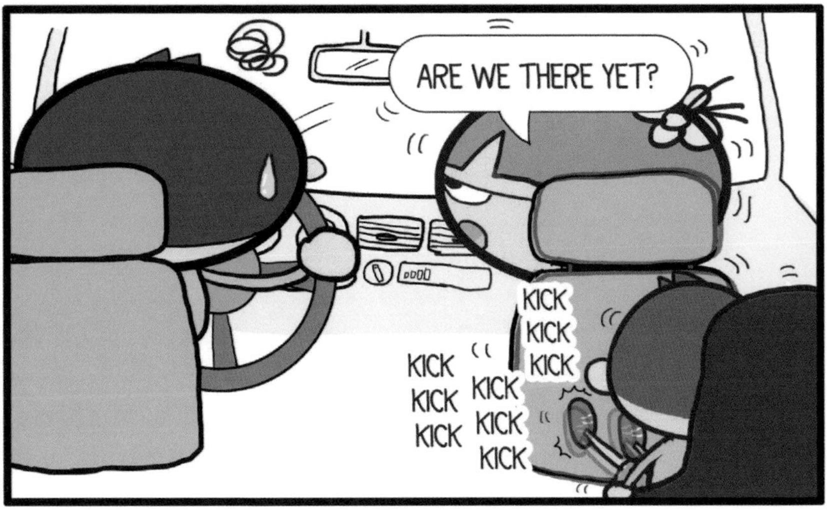
ARE WE THERE YET?
KICK
KICK
KICK
KICK
KICK
KICK
KICK
KICK
KICK

BEDTIME COMPANION

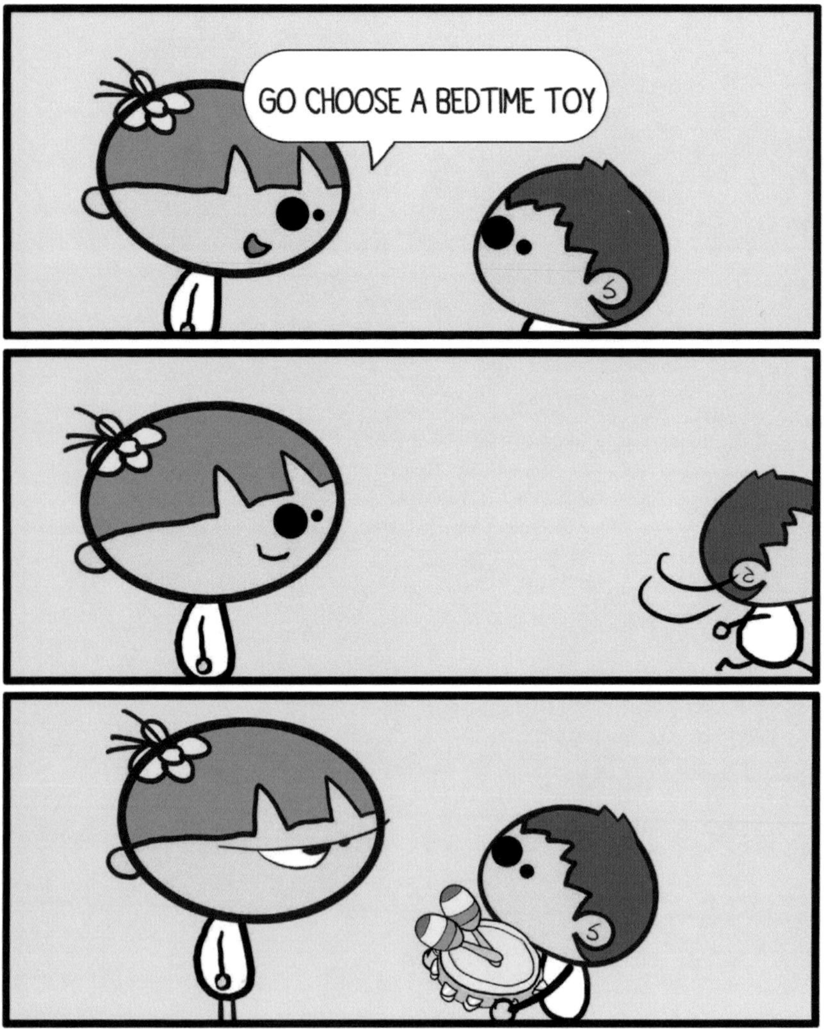
GO CHOOSE A BEDTIME TOY

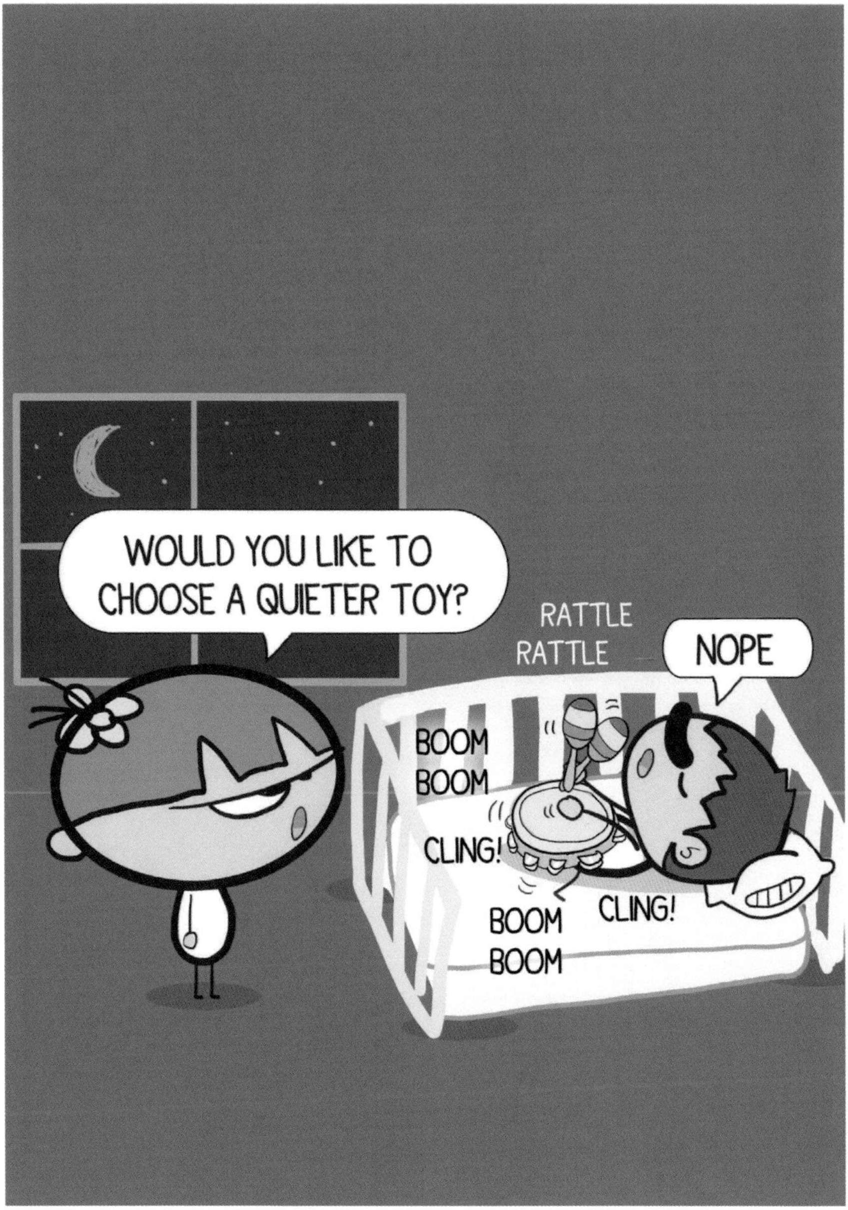
WOULD YOU LIKE TO CHOOSE A QUIETER TOY?
RATTLE RATTLE
NOPE
BOOM BOOM
CLING!
BOOM BOOM
CLING!

REALLY?

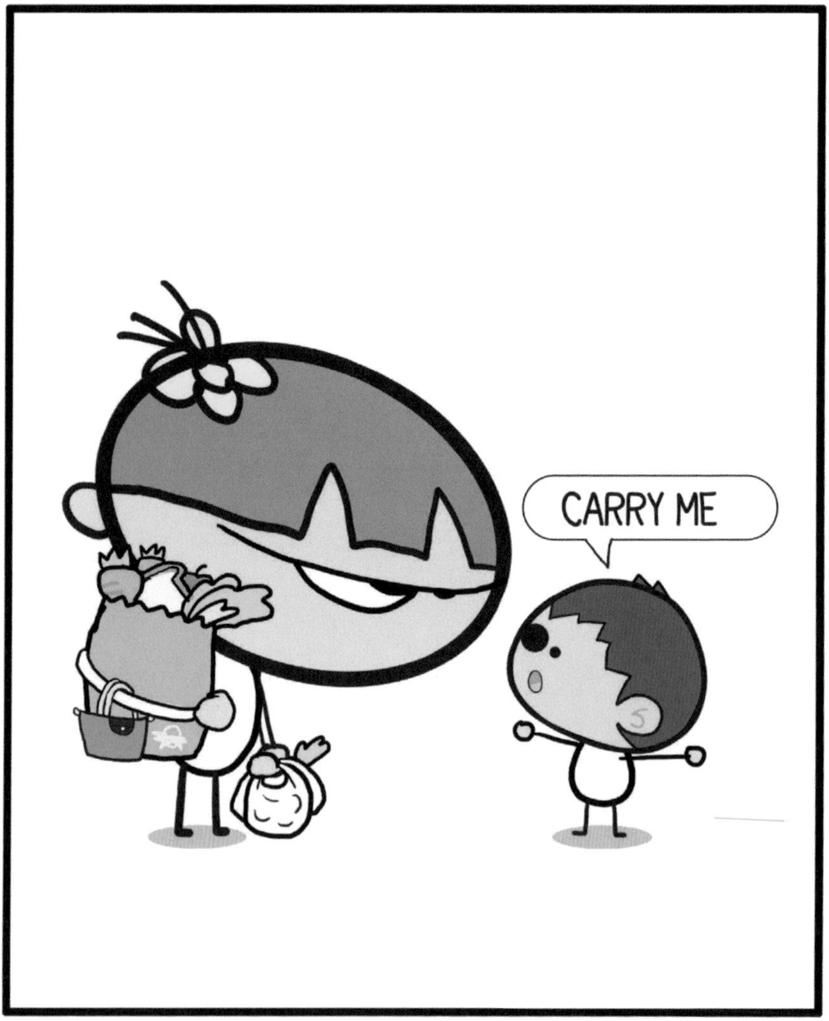
CARRY ME

HIS OWN DECISION

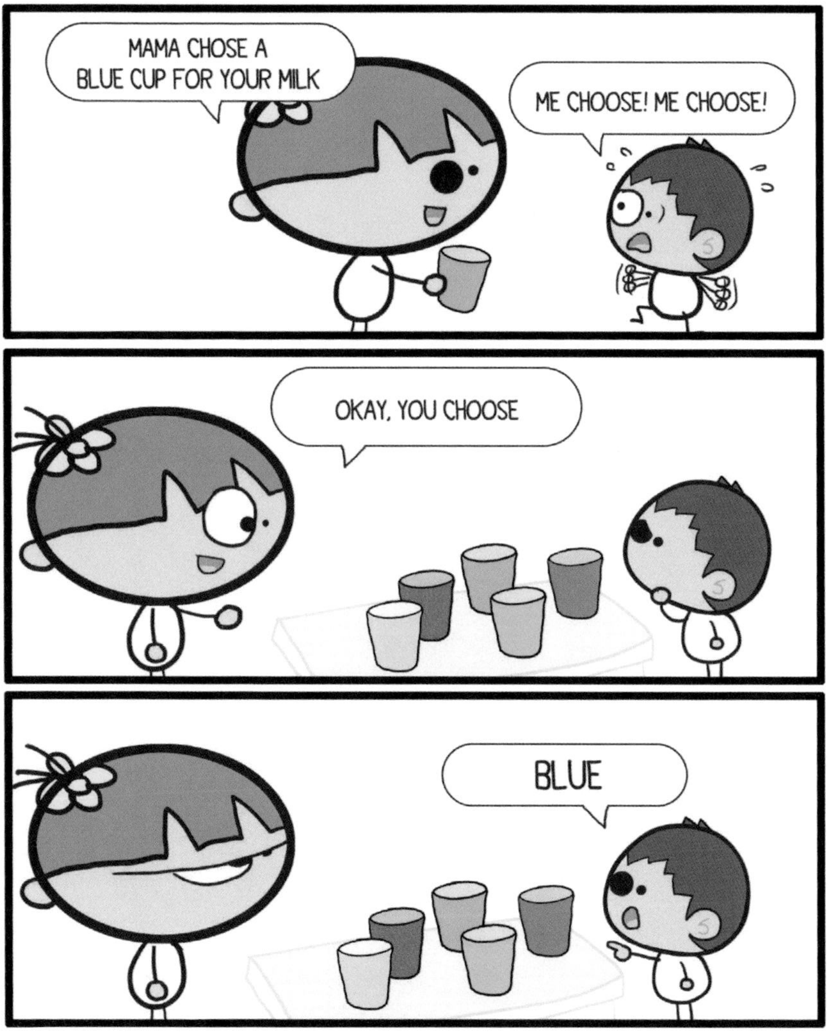
MAMA CHOSE A BLUE CUP FOR YOUR MILK
ME CHOOSE! ME CHOOSE!
OKAY, YOU CHOOSE
BLUE

HOUSE CLEANING

MOP
MOP
MOP
VROOM
VROOM
VROOM
NOM
NOM
NOM

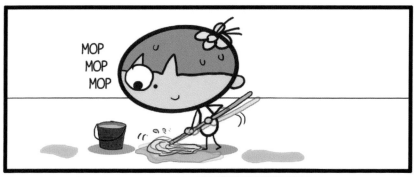

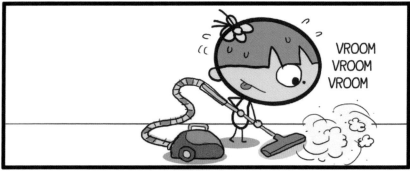

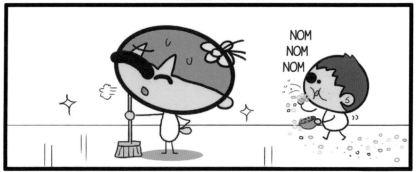

YES, I KNOW

WOW, WHAT'S THIS?
WOOD

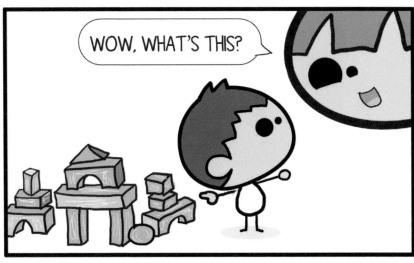

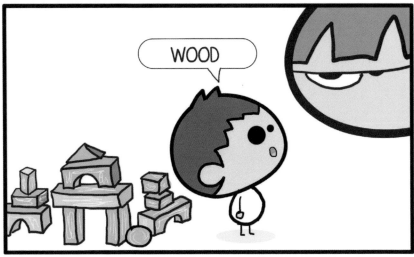

PUBLIC BATHROOMS

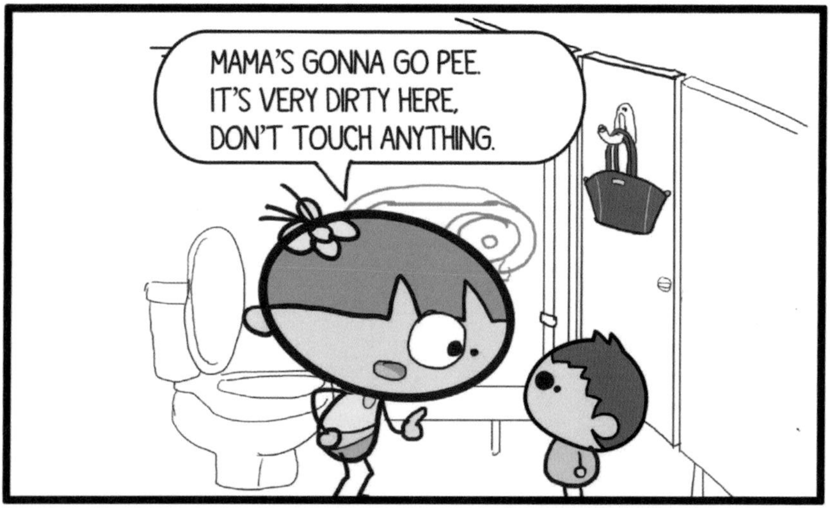
MAMA'S GONNA GO PEE.
IT'S VERY DIRTY HERE,
DON'T TOUCH ANYTHING.

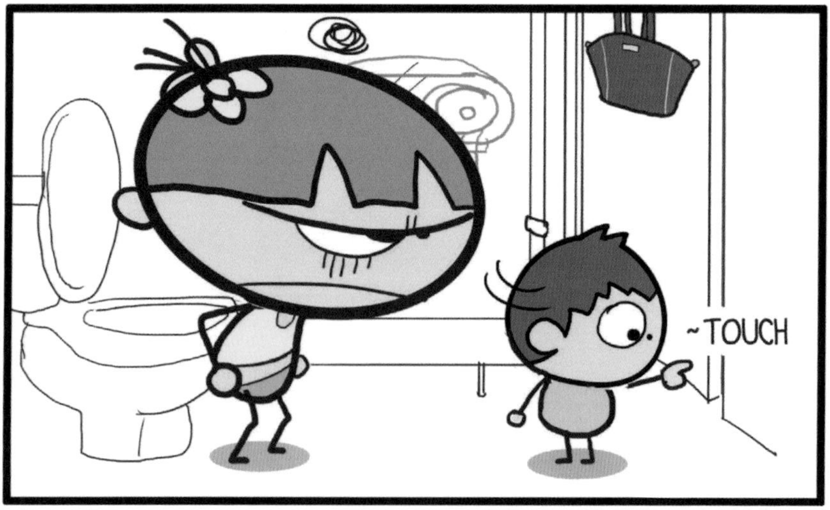
~TOUCH

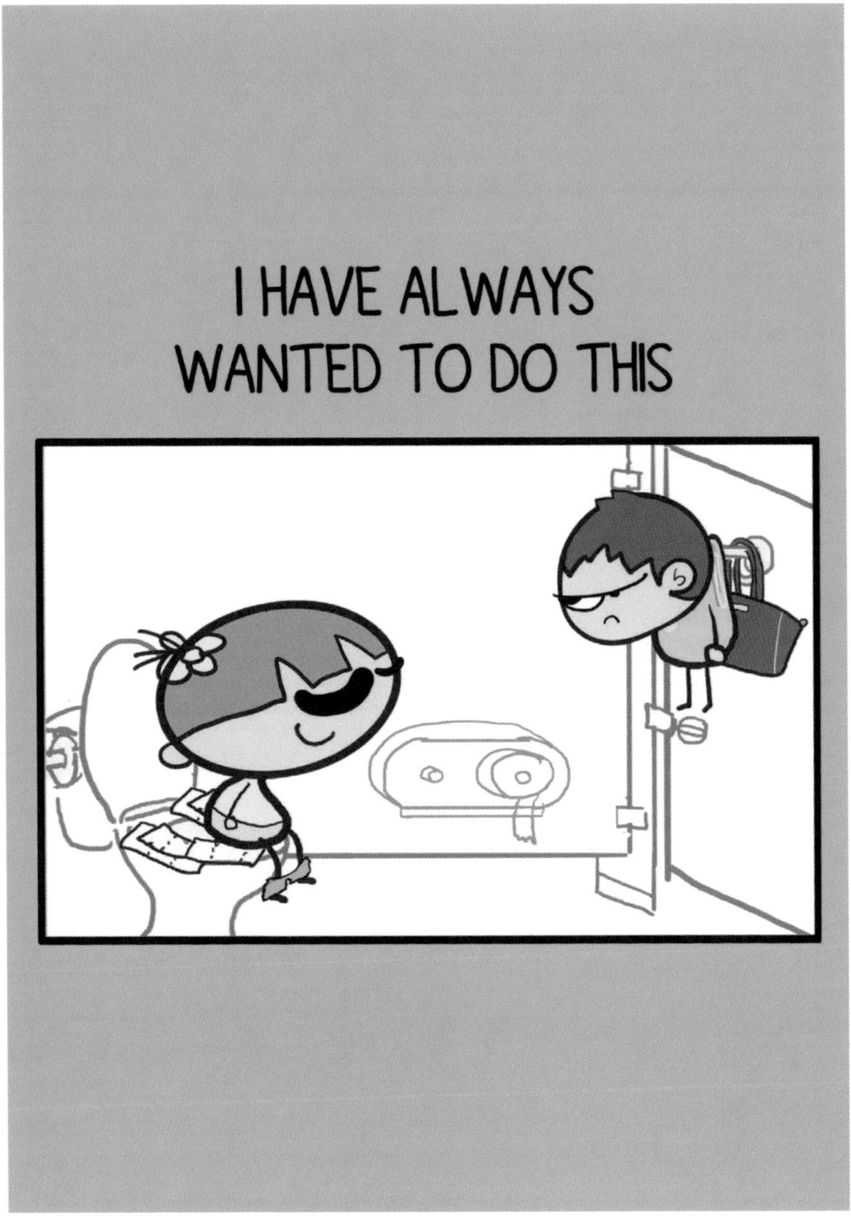
I HAVE ALWAYS
WANTED TO DO THIS

PROTEST

WHY IS HE CRYING?
BECAUSE HE WANTS TO STICK HIS FINGER UP MY NOSE AND I SAID NO.

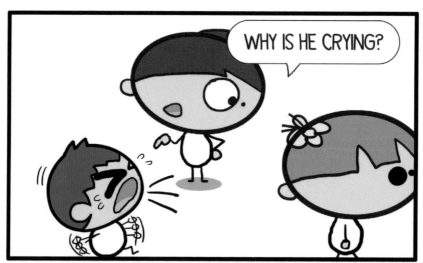

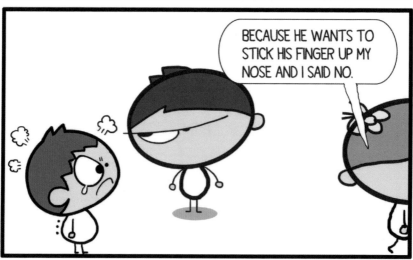

AS IF NOTHING HAPPENED

DID YOU JUST POOP?
NOPE

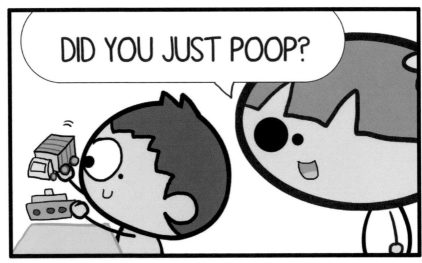

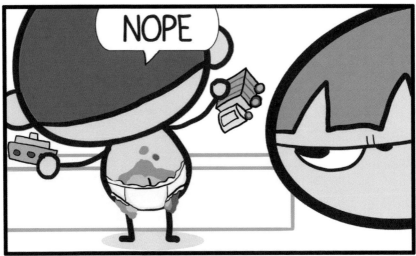

FAVORITE FOOD

WHAT CAN I GET YOU FOLKS TONIGHT?
OUR DINNER SPECIAL IS STEAK AND CAJUN SHRIMP SERVED WITH ASPARAGUS AND HOLLANDAISE SAUCE
BREAD

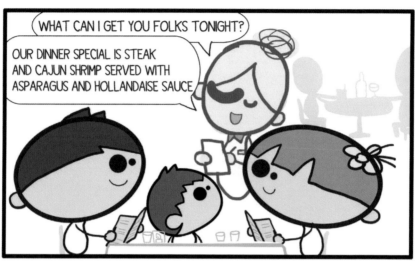

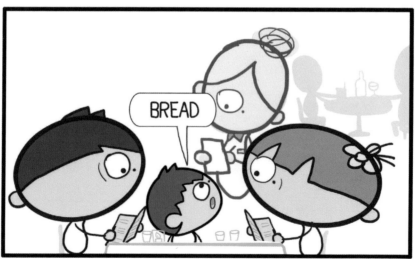

DRAWING

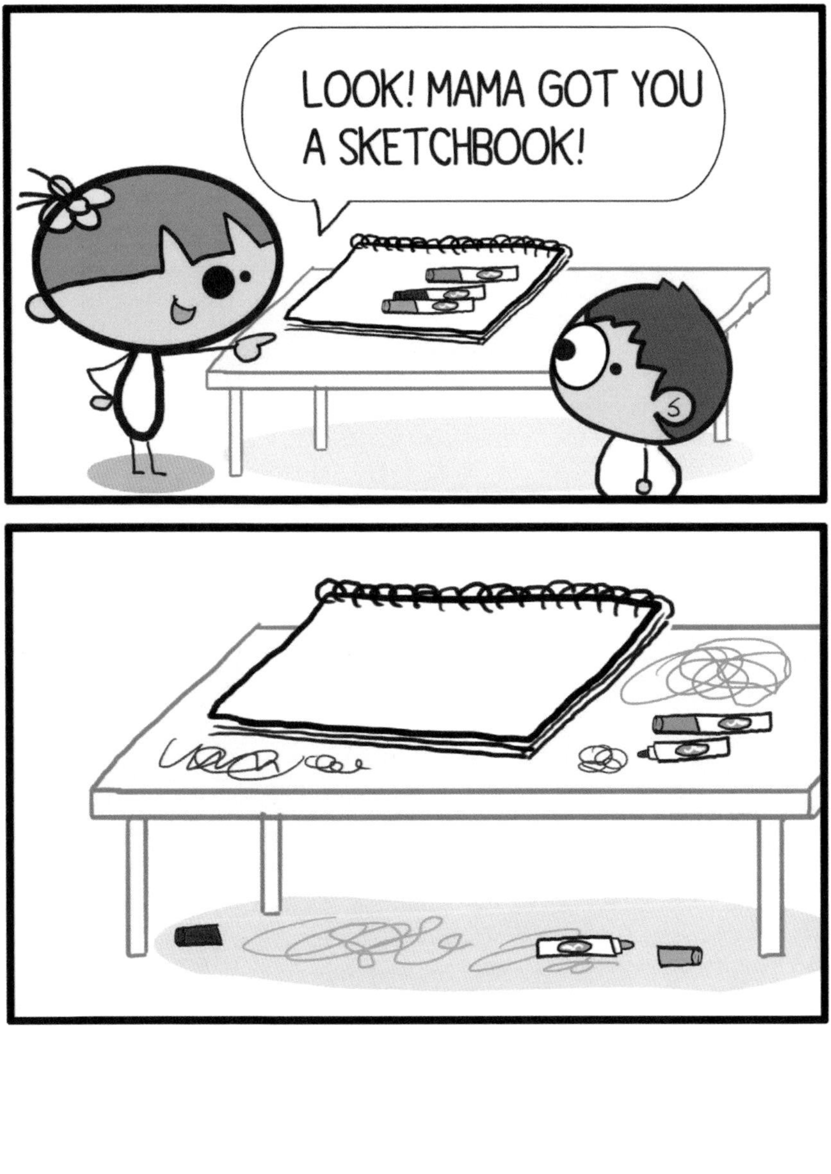
LOOK! MAMA GOT YOU A SKETCHBOOK!

PRIORITIES

CHATTING WITH THE DAYCARE TEACHER
TODAY, YOUR CHILD DID SOME READING, DRAWING AND SINGING
JUST TELL ME IF HE DID ANY EATING, SLEEPING AND POOPING

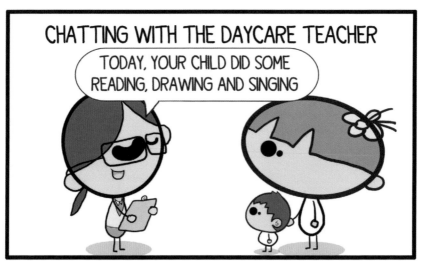

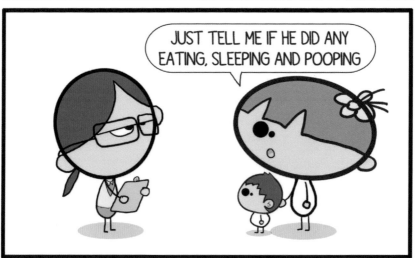

DRUMS

MAMA GOT YOU A DRUM!
TRY IT!
BANG
STOP IT
BANG
BANG
BANG
STOP IT
BANG
BANG
BANG
BANG
BANG
BANG
BANG
STOP IT!!!!

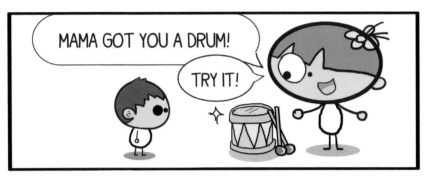

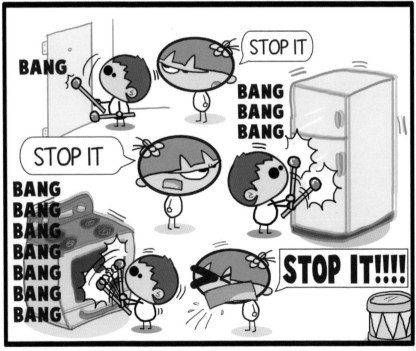

FIRST WORD

!
SH*T!
SH*T!

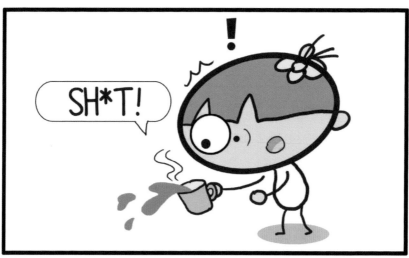

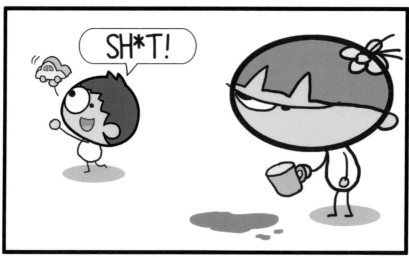

READING TIME

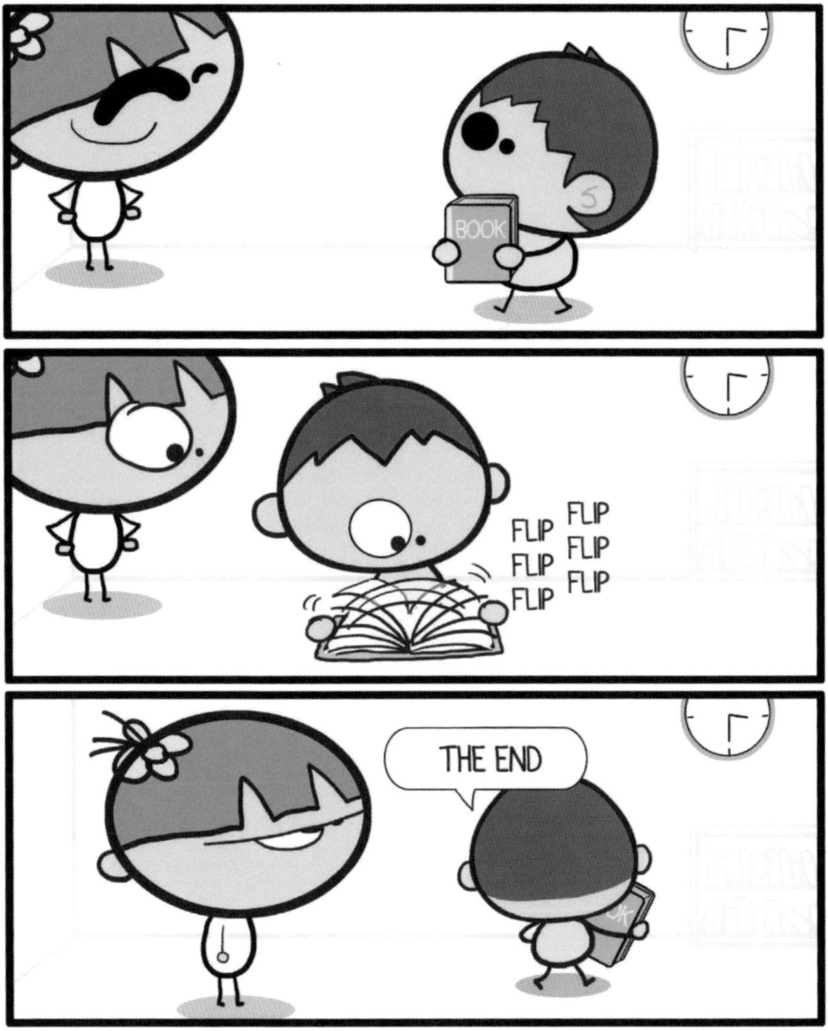
BOOK
FLIP FLIP FLIP FLIP FLIP FLIP
THE END

I WANT MY MONEY BACK

MAMA!
MAMA!
MAMA!
MAMA!

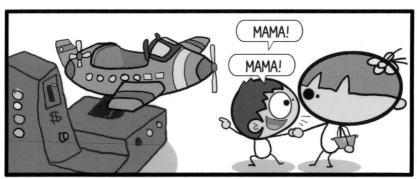

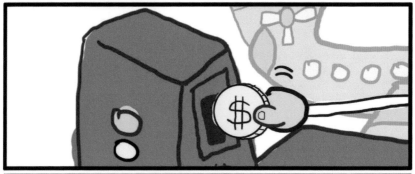

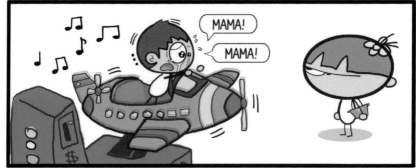

A GIFT FROM MY SON

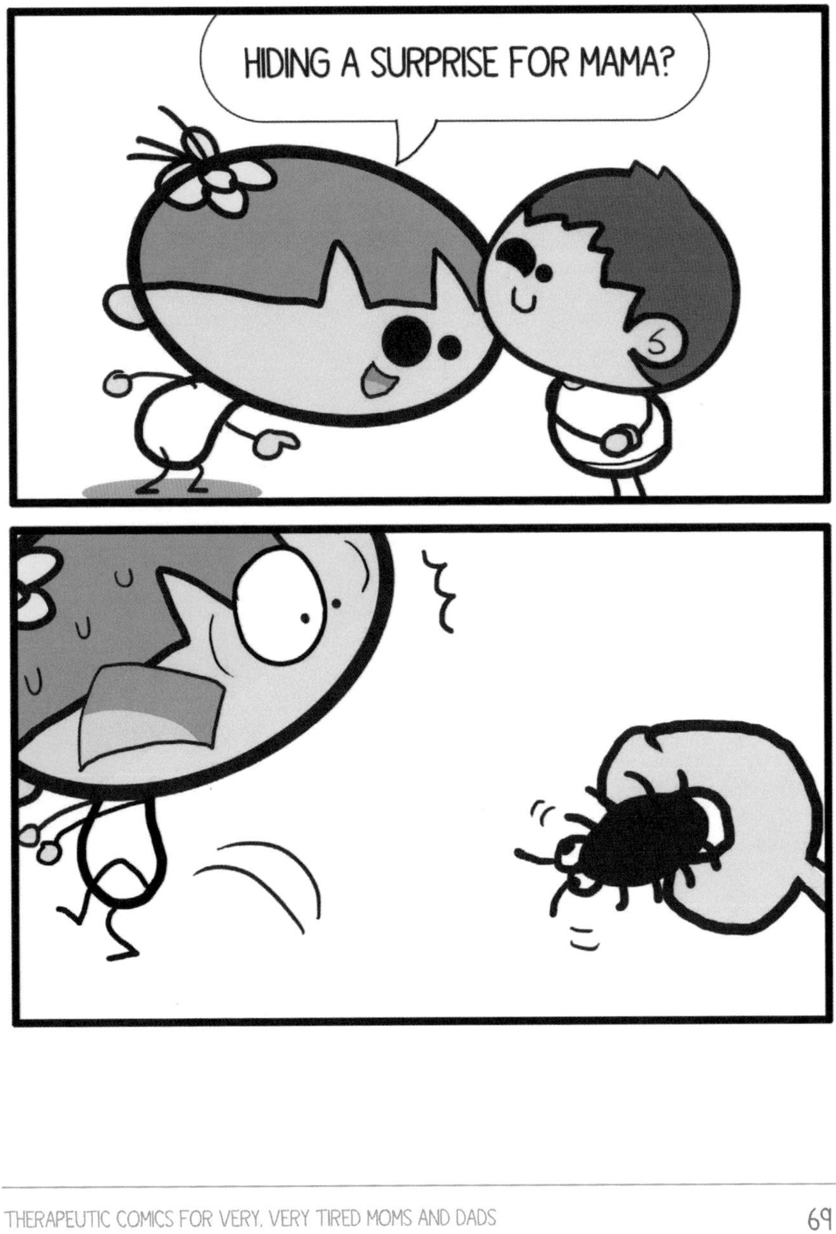
HIDING A SURPRISE FOR MAMA?

GUYS NIGHT OUT

I'M GOING OUT NOW!
CAN I COME TOO?
SORRY, BOYS ONLY
OK, TAKE HIM

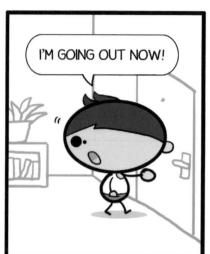

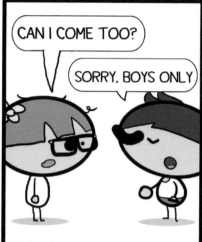

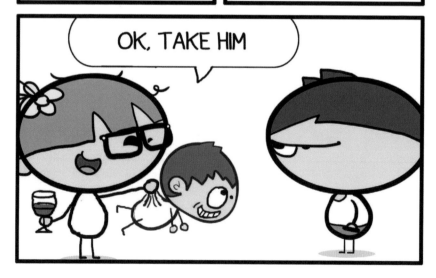

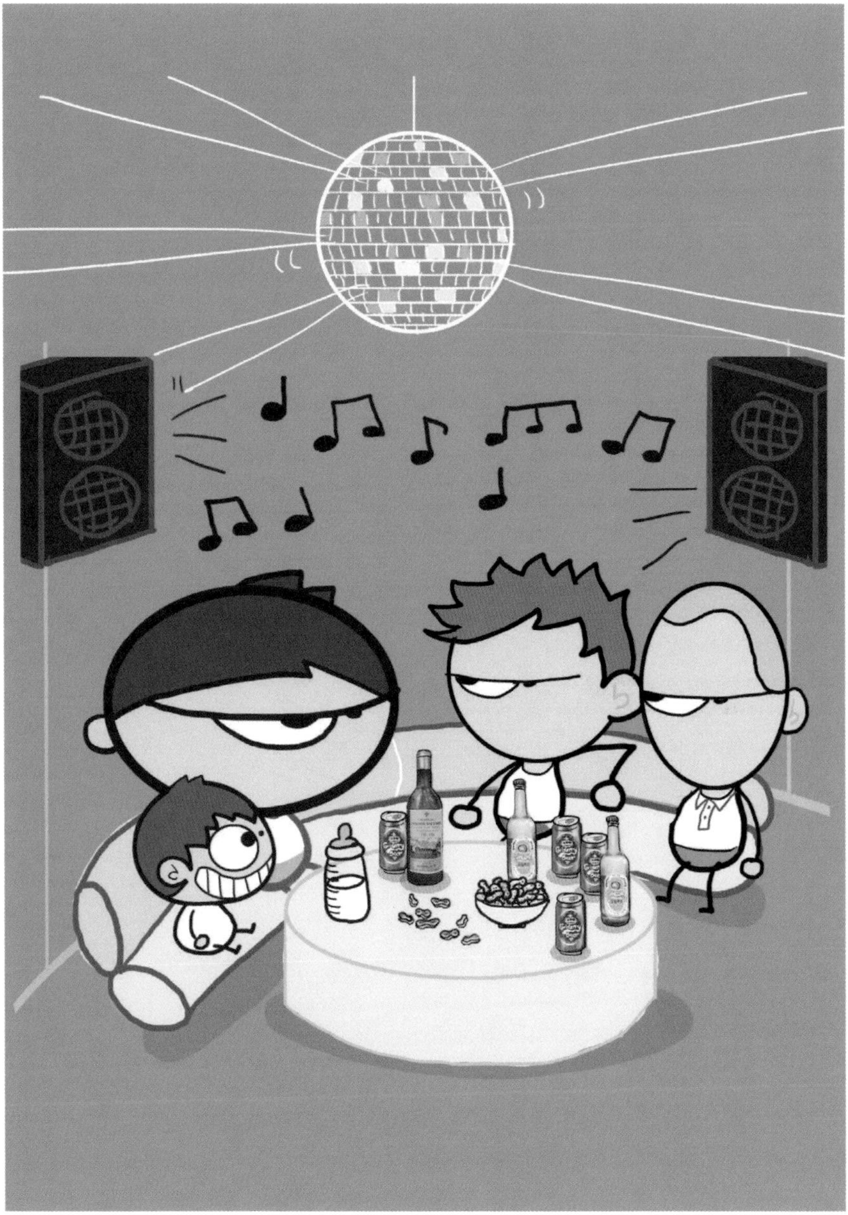

HOW'S IT GOING?

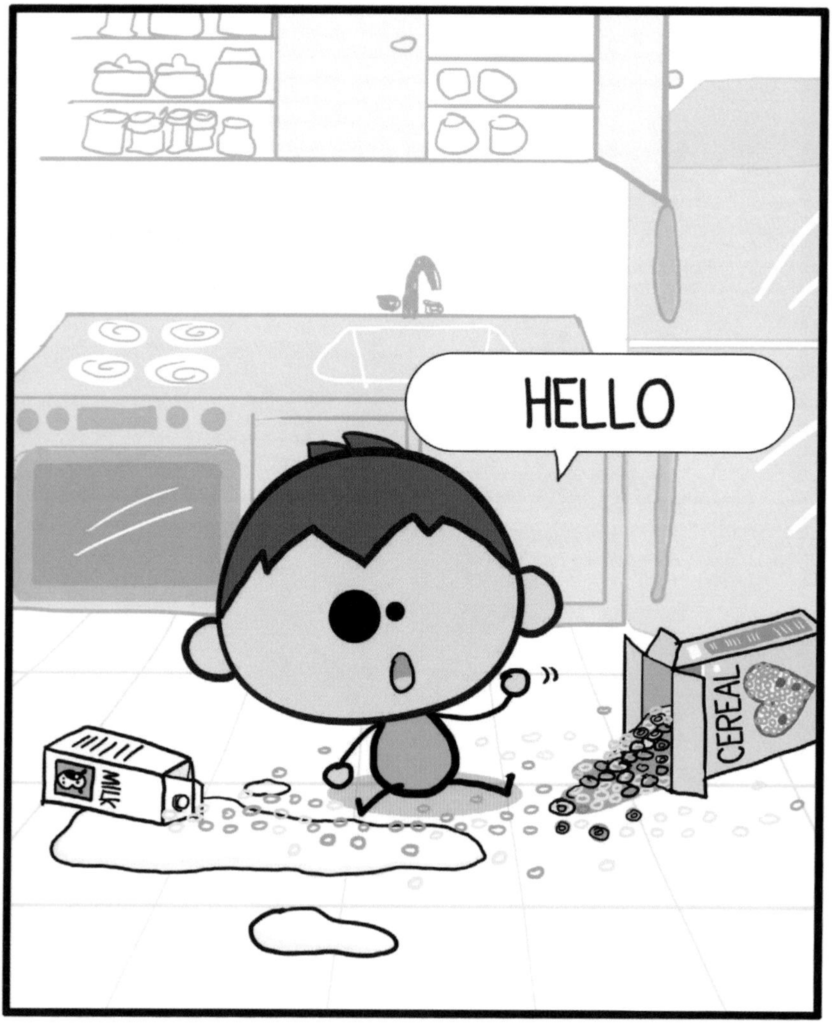
HELLO
MILK
CEREAL

I'M NOW INVISIBLE

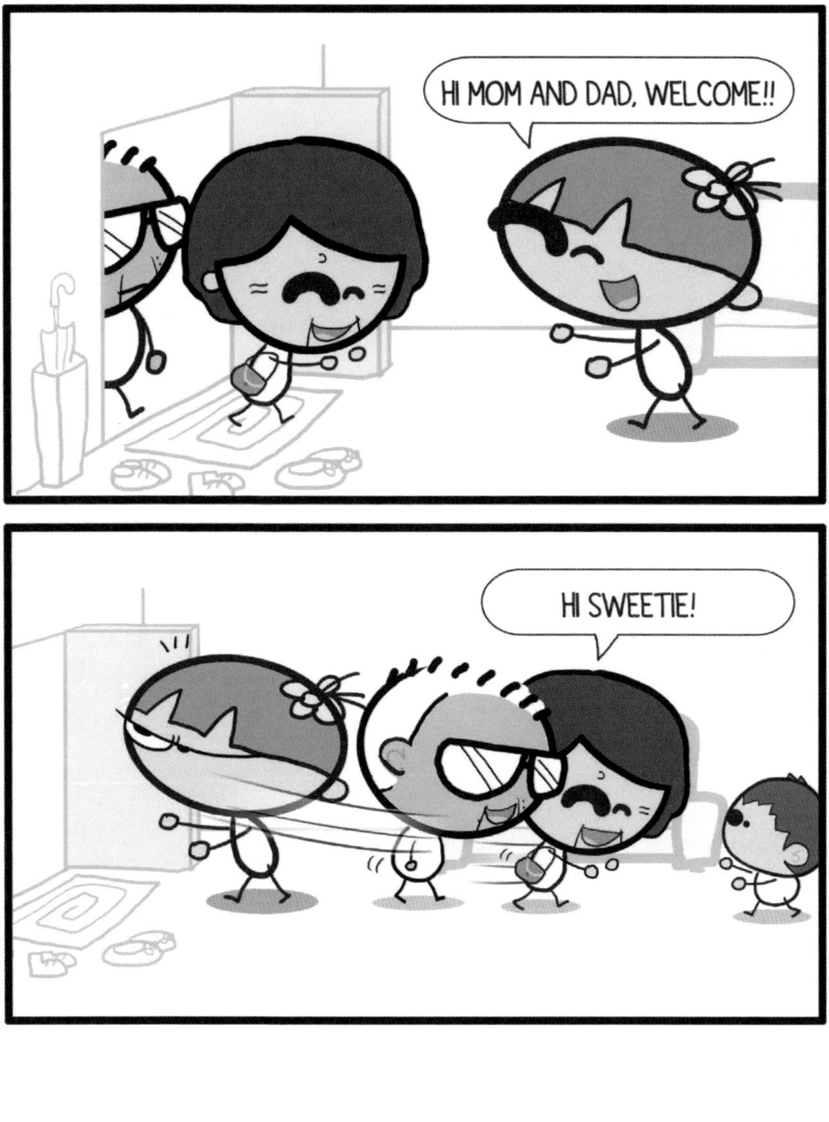
HI MOM AND DAD, WELCOME!!
HI SWEETIE!

CLEAN UP

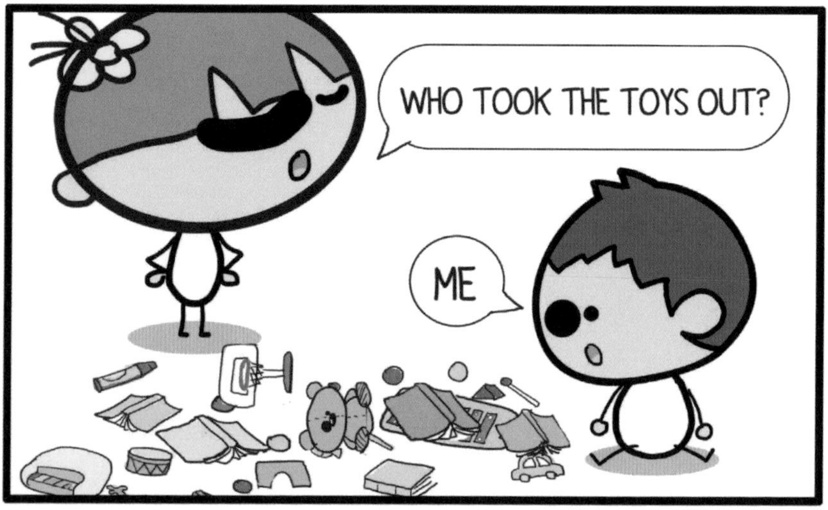
WHO TOOK THE TOYS OUT?
ME

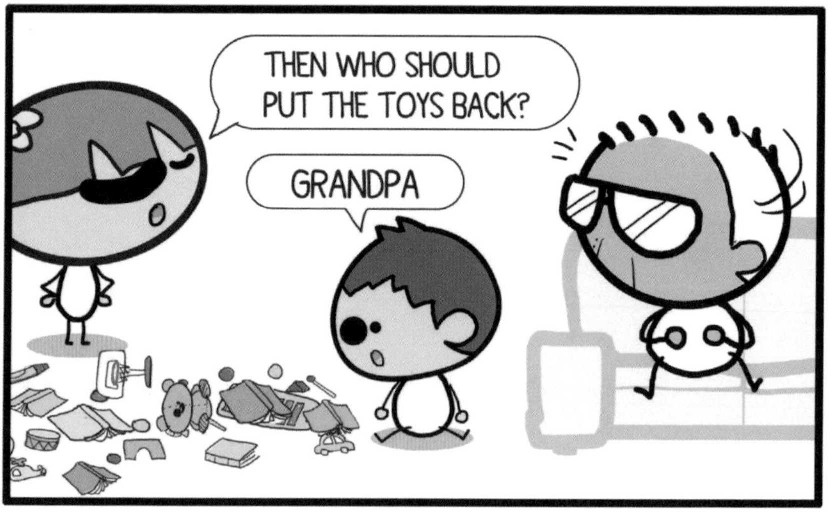
THEN WHO SHOULD PUT THE TOYS BACK?
GRANDPA

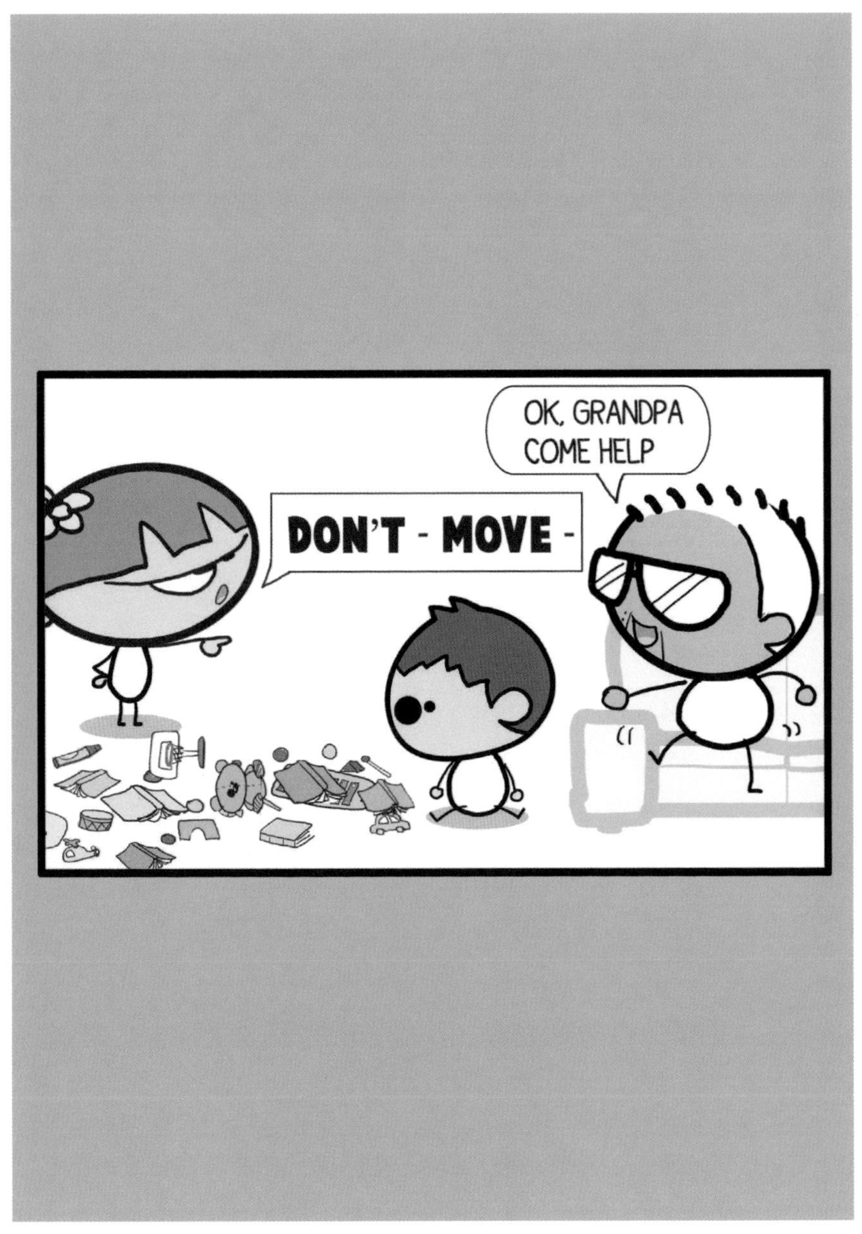
DON'T - MOVE -
OK, GRANDPA
COME HELP

ESCAPE FAILED

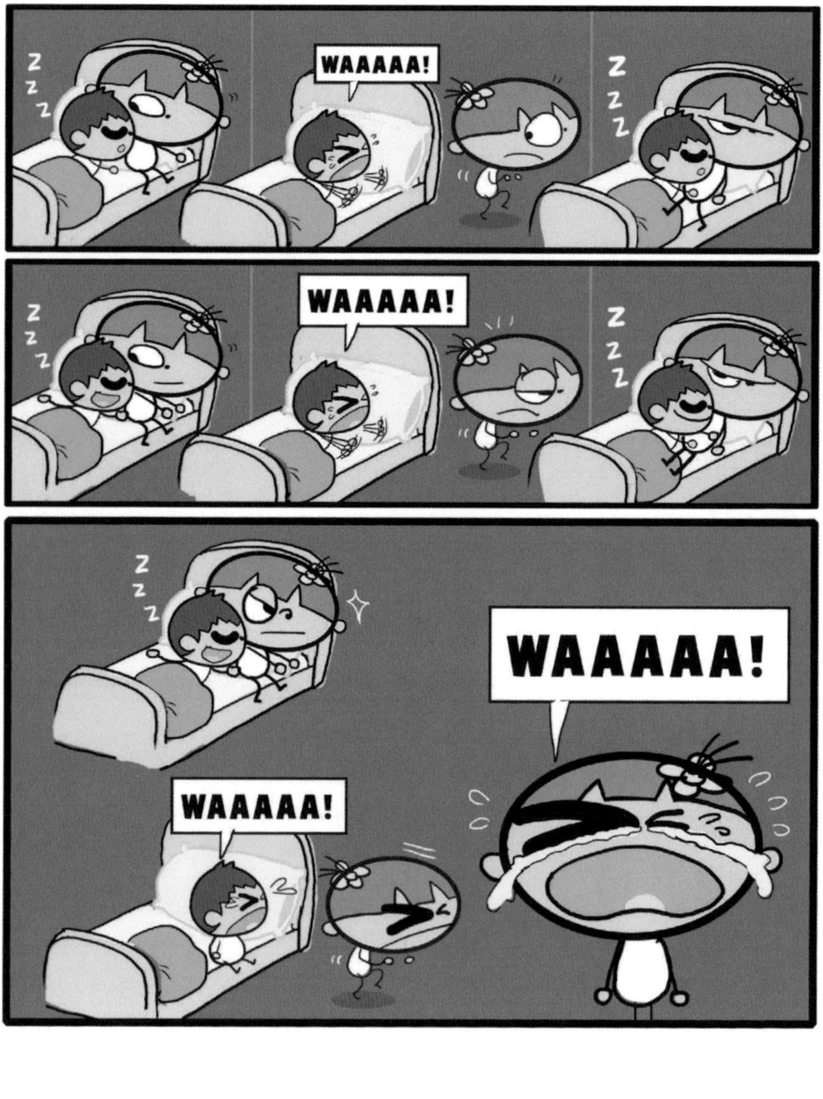
Z
Z
Z
WAAAAA!
Z
Z
Z
Z
Z
Z
WAAAAA!
Z
Z
Z
Z
Z
Z
WAAAAA!
WAAAAA!

OK, MY TURN

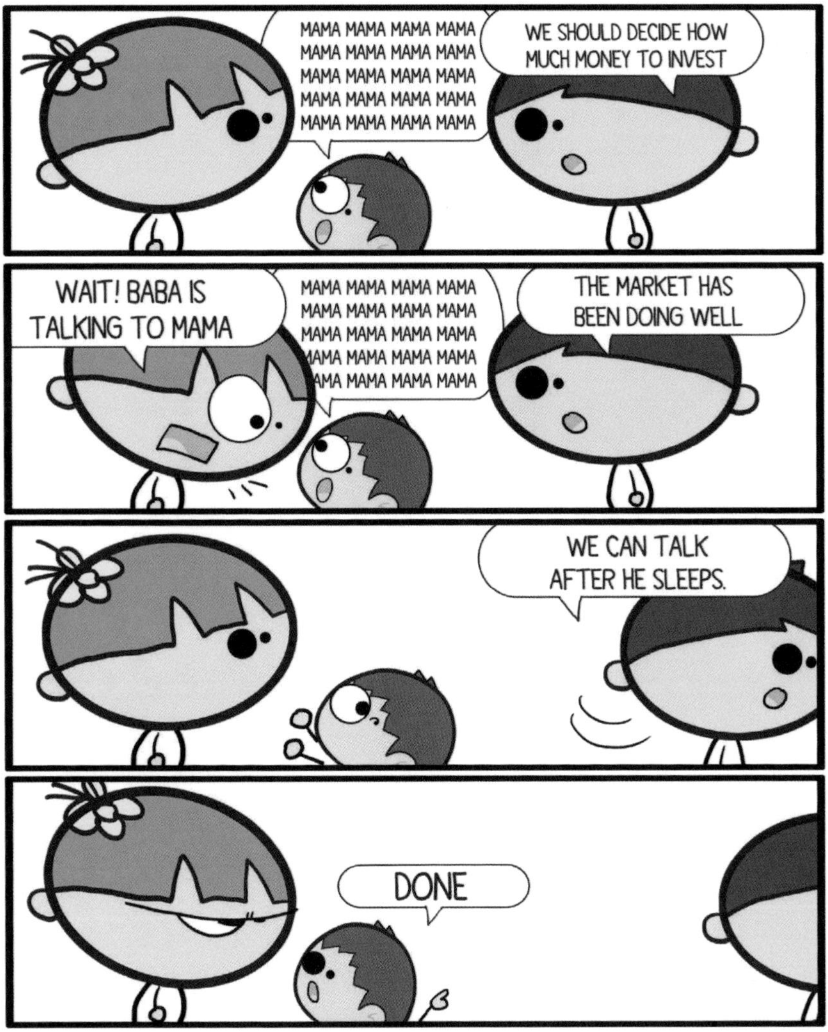
MAMA MAMA MAMA MAMA MAMA MAMA MAMA MAMA MAMA MAMA MAMA MAMA MAMA MAMA MAMA MAMA MAMA MAMA MAMA MAMA
WE SHOULD DECIDE HOW MUCH MONEY TO INVEST
WAIT! BABA IS TALKING TO MAMA
MAMA MAMA MAMA MAMA MAMA MAMA MAMA MAMA MAMA MAMA MAMA MAMA MAMA MAMA MAMA MAMA MAMA MAMA MAMA MAMA
THE MARKET HAS BEEN DOING WELL
WE CAN TALK AFTER HE SLEEPS.
DONE

DIFFICULTY LEVEL OF A SIMPLE TASK: HIGH

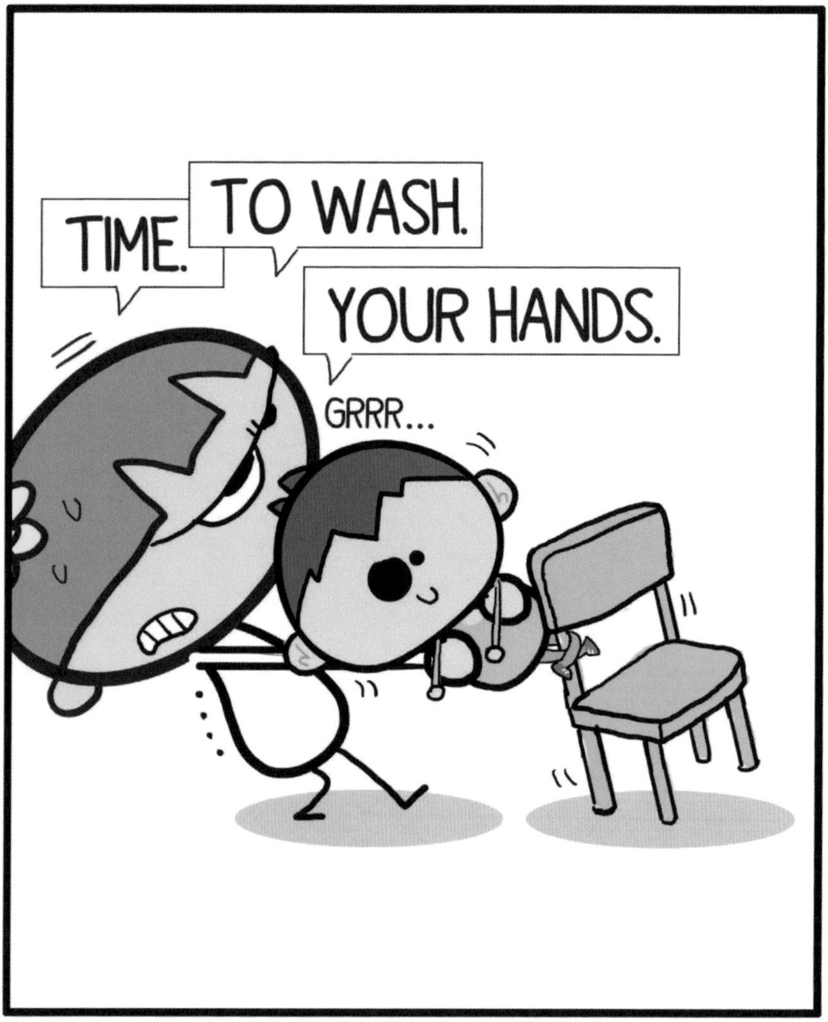
TIME.
TO WASH.
YOUR HANDS.
GRRR...

HOBBIES

WHAT DOES BABA ALWAYS DO?
SLEEP
WHAT DOES MAMA ALWAYS DO?
TALK

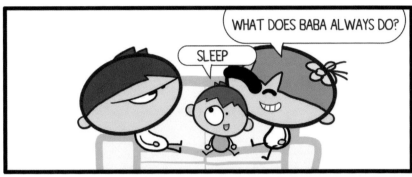

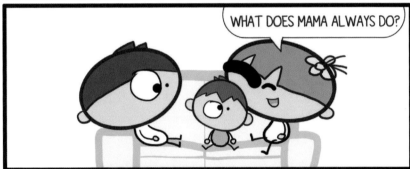

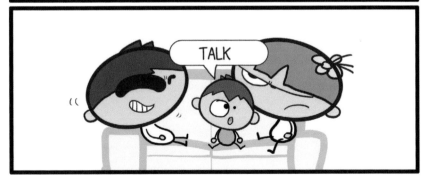

MY SON IN REAL LIFE
WAAA WAAA WAAA WAAA WAAA WAAA
MY SON ON SOCIAL MEDIA
Summer and Muu Comics
Like This Page · October 24
SO CUTE
Follow me on IG:
https://www.instagram.com/summerandmuu/
Tag Photo
Tag Products
Add Location
Edit
2456257 people reached
Boost Post
Like
Comment
Share
3.5K
Chronological
40,182 Shares
View previous comments
Harry Baals adorable!
Like · Reply · Message
Heidi Ho He is so cute and well behaved!
Like · Reply · Message
3 Replies
B. Obama Look at those duck lips!
Like · Reply · Message
Justin Case handsome boy
HOME SWEET

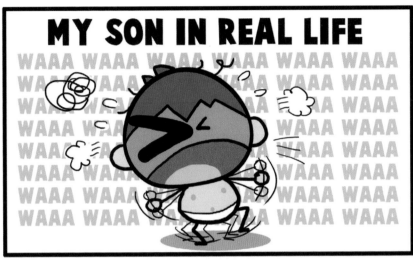

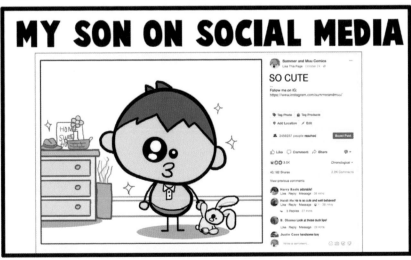

NO MELTDOWN!

TODAY WAS A LONG DAY AT THE AMUSEMENT PARK AND HE DIDN'T HAVE A MELTDOWN!
THAT'S MY GRANDSON!
NO I MEANT MY HUSBAND DIDN'T HAVE A MELTDOWN.

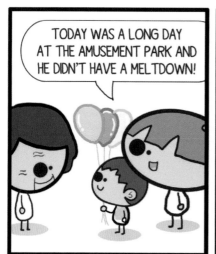

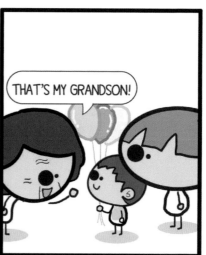

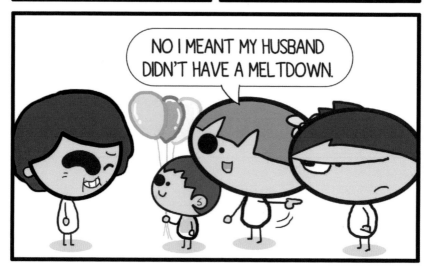

PAUSE

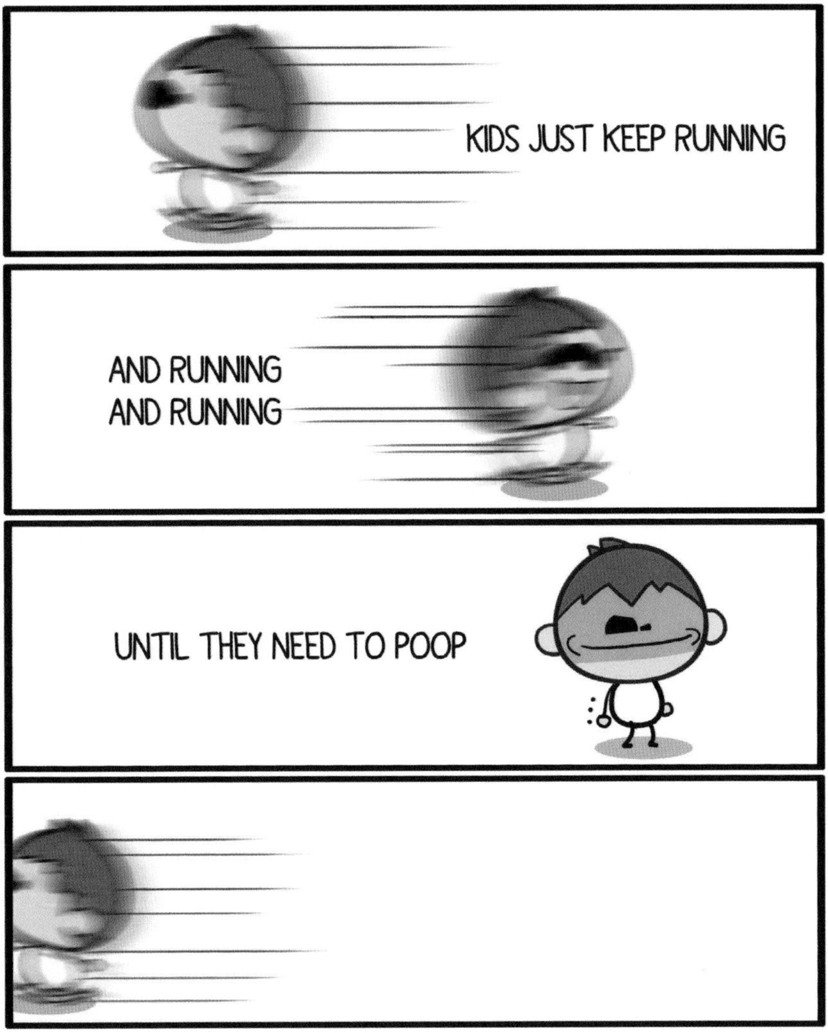
KIDS JUST KEEP RUNNING
AND RUNNING
AND RUNNING
UNTIL THEY NEED TO POOP

NEGOTIATING

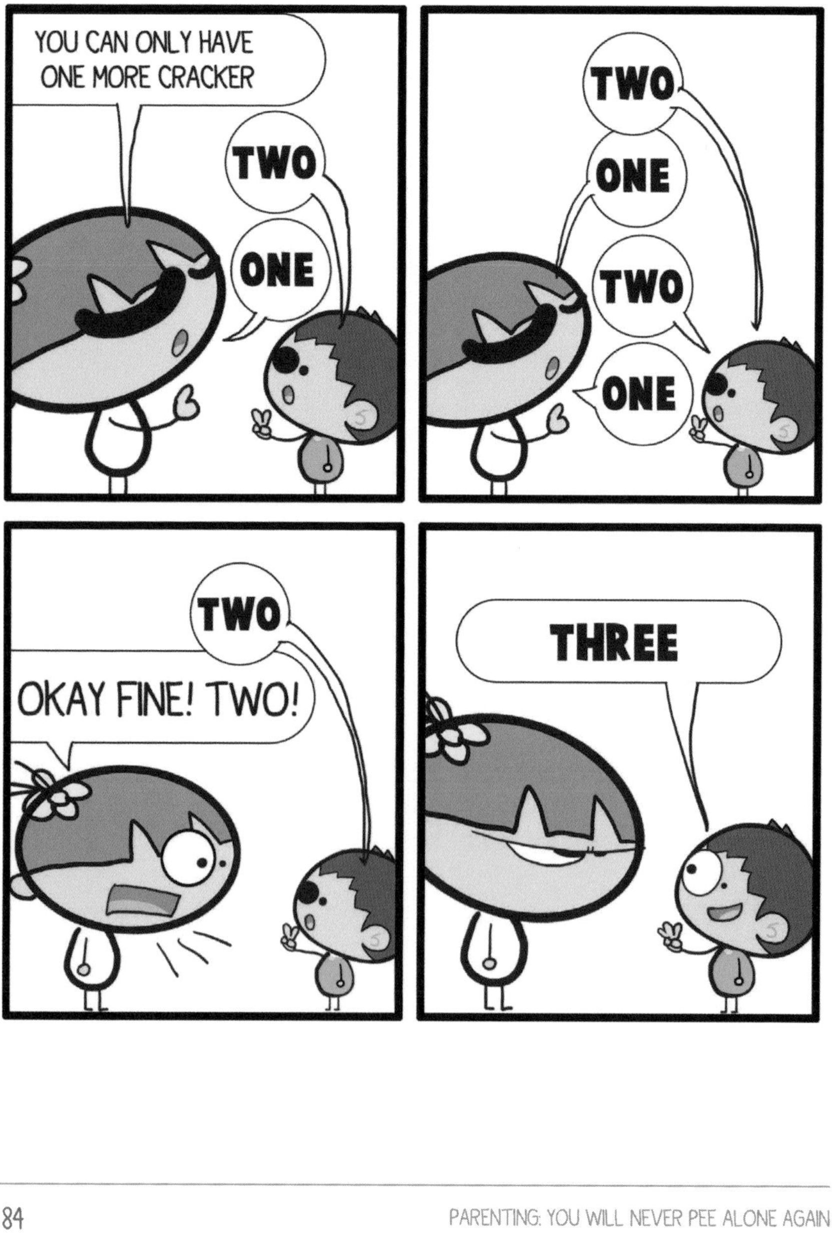
YOU CAN ONLY HAVE ONE MORE CRACKER
TWO
ONE
TWO
ONE
TWO
ONE
TWO
OKAY FINE! TWO!
THREE

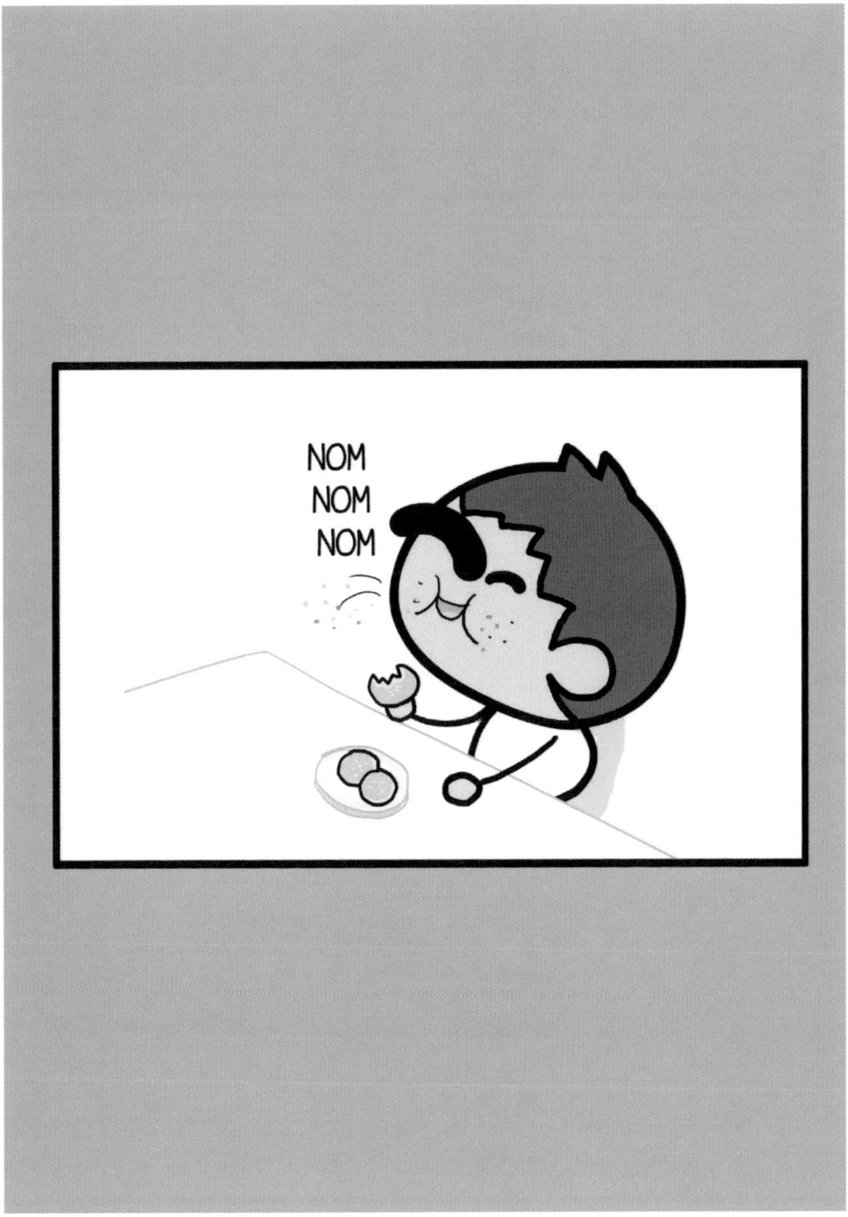
NOM
NOM
NOM

GOING TO THE PARK

DO YOU WANNA GO TO THE PARK?
YES
AND PLAY ON THE SLIDES?
YES
AND GO UP THE SWINGS??
YES!
THEN PUT YOUR PANTS ON AND LET'S GO
NO

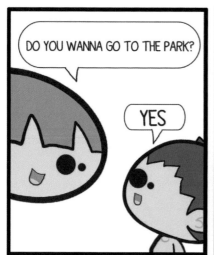

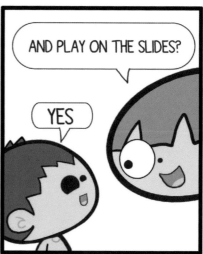

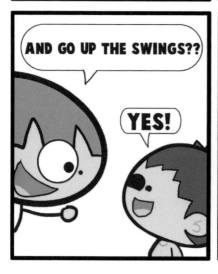

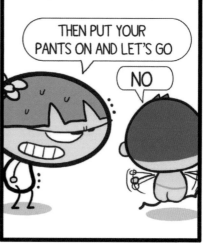

LITTLE BRAT

MAMA IS TALKING TO YOU, YOU NEED TO LOOK ME IN THE EYES
!
POKE~

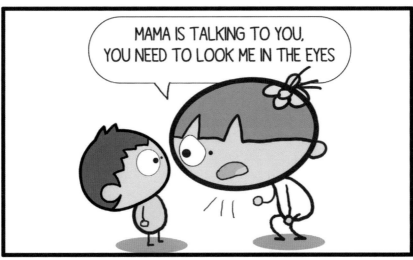

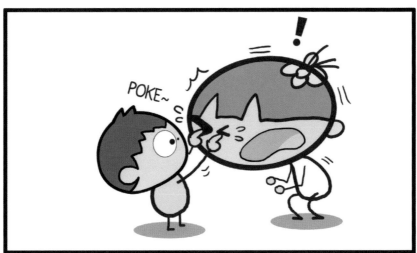

NEVER GIVE UP

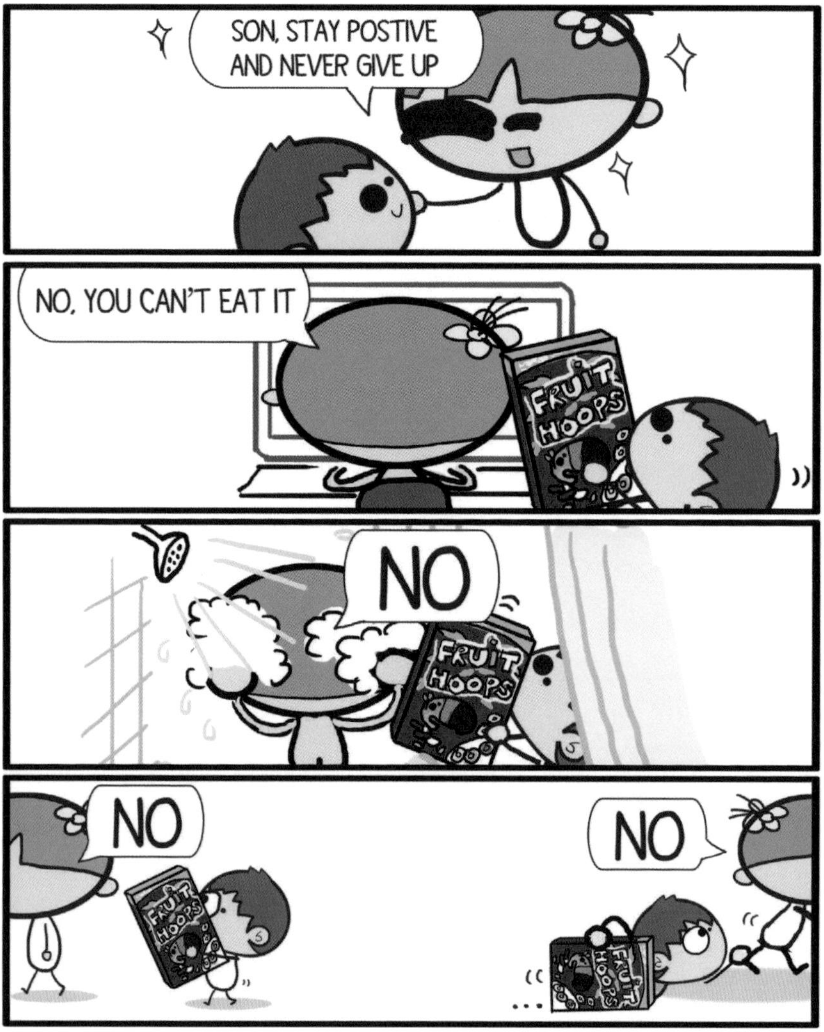
SON, STAY POSTIVE AND NEVER GIVE UP
NO, YOU CAN'T EAT IT
FRUIT HOOPS
NO
FRUIT HOOPS
NO
FRUIT HOOPS
NO
FRUIT HOOPS

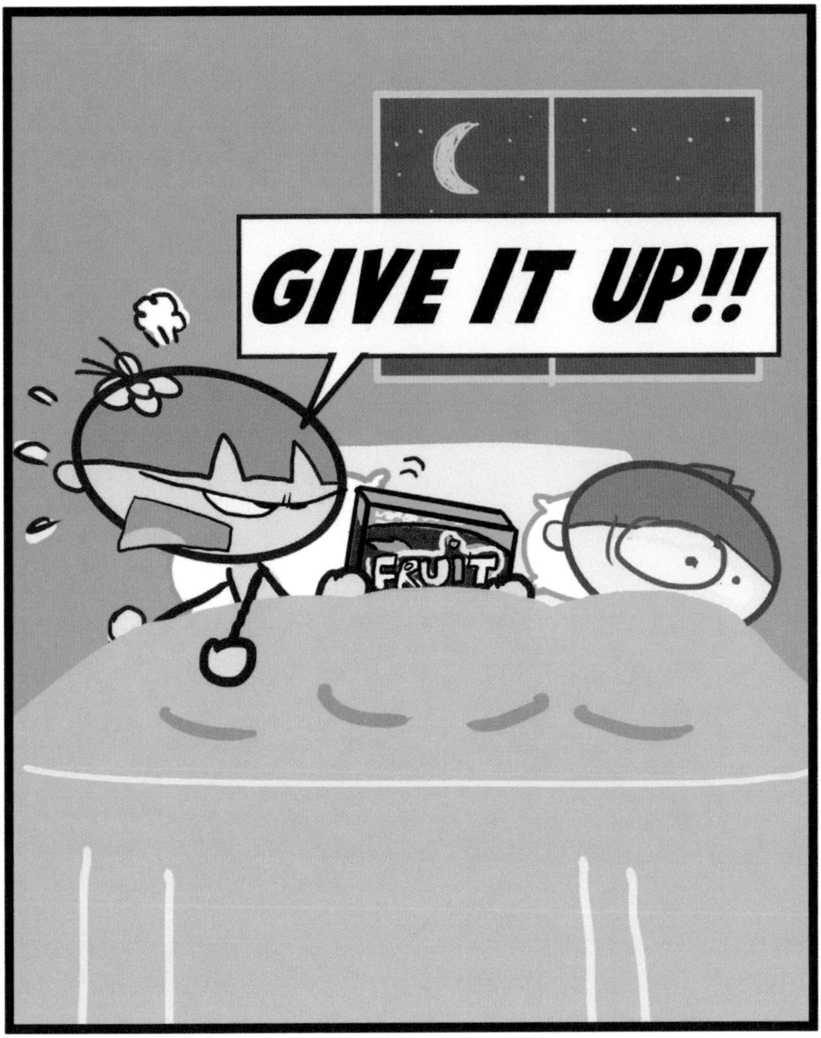
GIVE IT UP!!
FRUIT

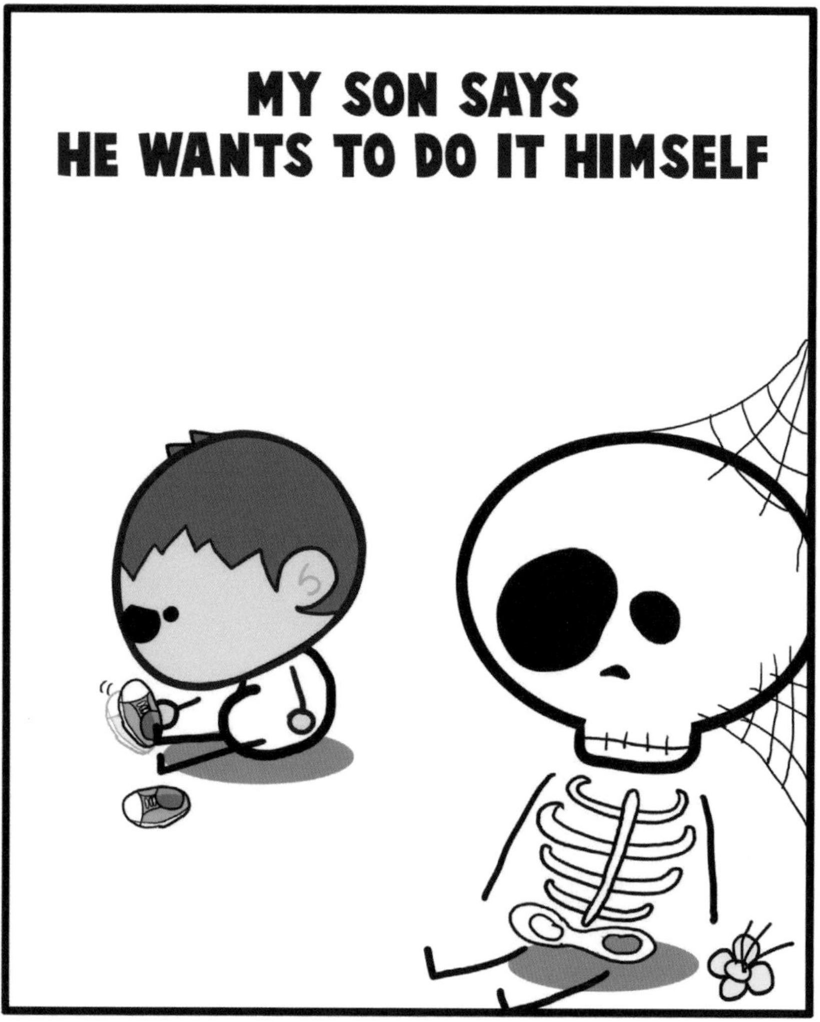
MY SON SAYS
HE WANTS TO DO IT HIMSELF

SOMETIMES YOU JUST HAVE TO GIVE UP

CAREFUL, MAMA SPILLED SOMETHING. DON'T STEP ON IT.

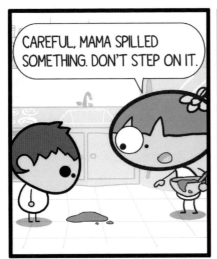

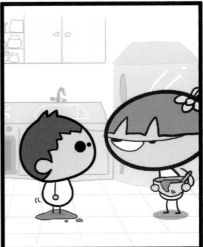

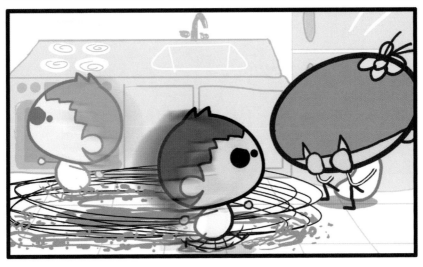

SLIPPERY WHEN WET

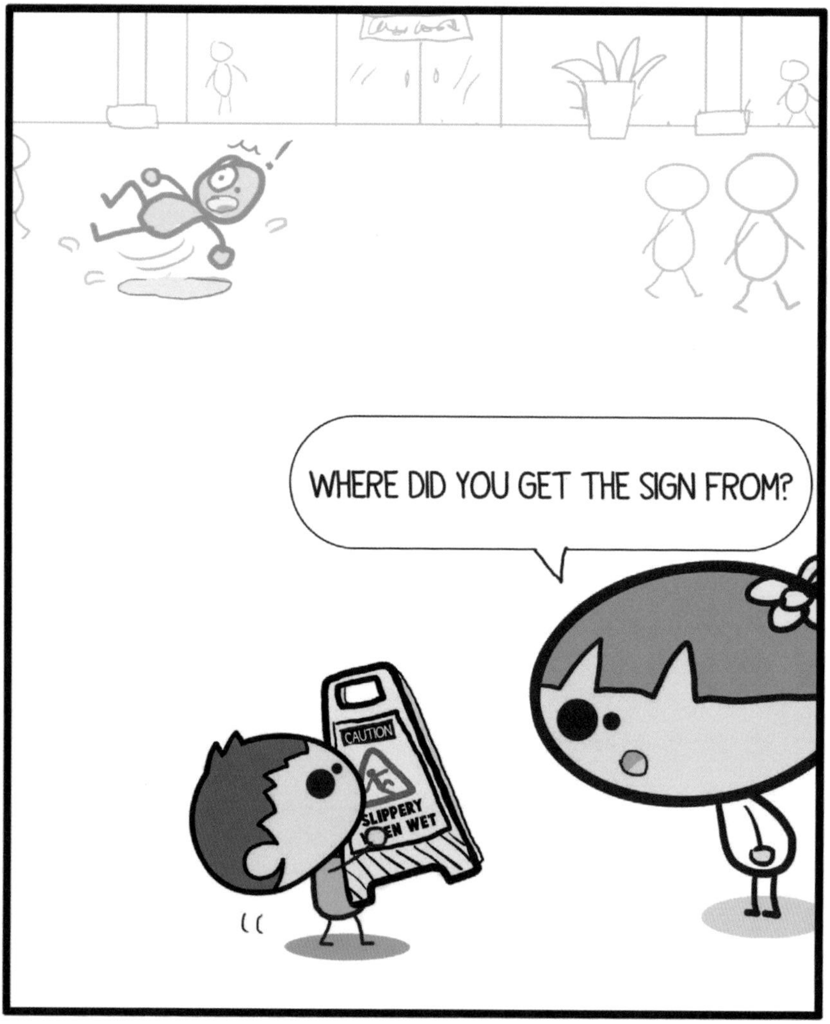
WHERE DID YOU GET THE SIGN FROM?
CAUTION
SLIPPERY
WHEN WET

HIS FAVORITE PLACE FOR STICKERS

MAMA GOT YOU A STICKER BOOK FOR YOUR STICKERS!

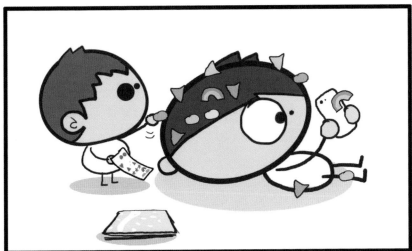

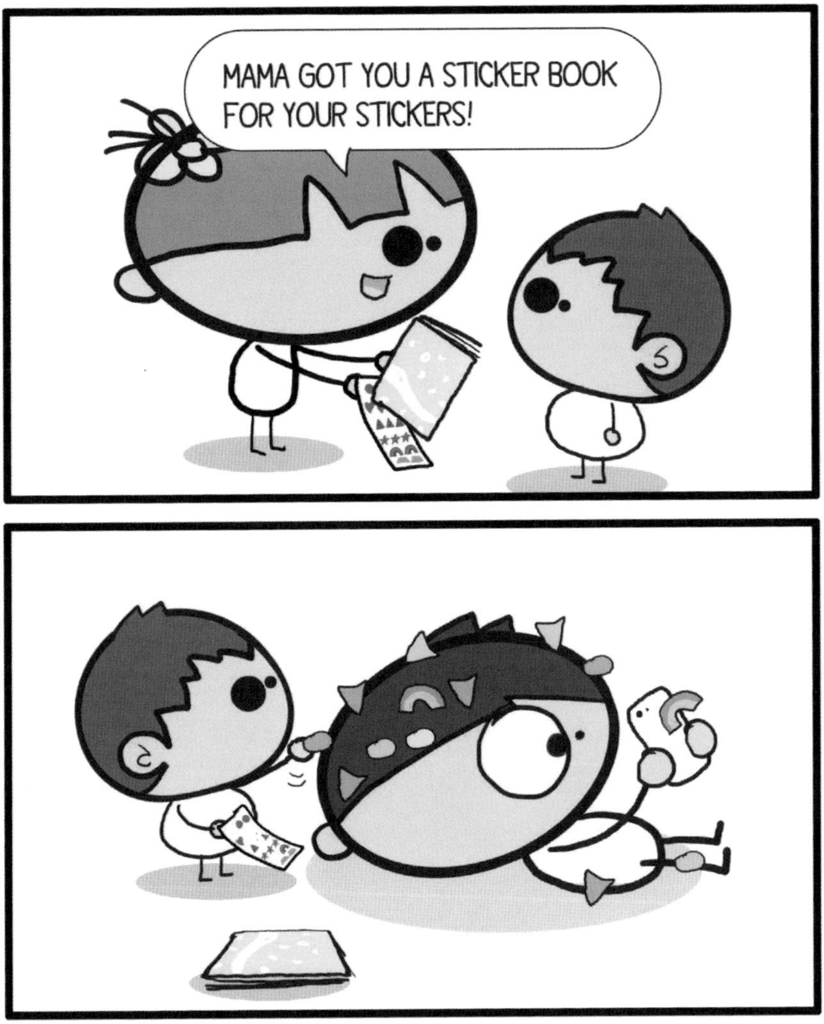

NAP TIME

HEY, WE'RE GONNA BE A BIT LATE
YA, SORRY, HE IS STILL NAPPING
OK, WE WILL HEAD OUT AS SOON AS WE CAN!
Z
Z
Z

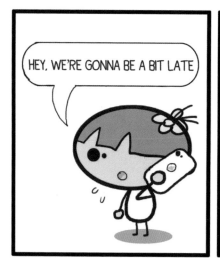

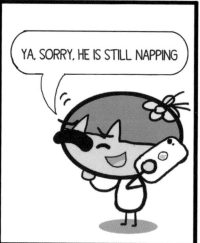

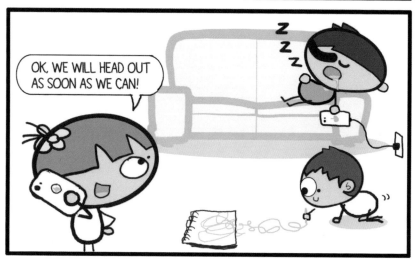

I SWEAR THEY DO THIS TO ANNOY YOU

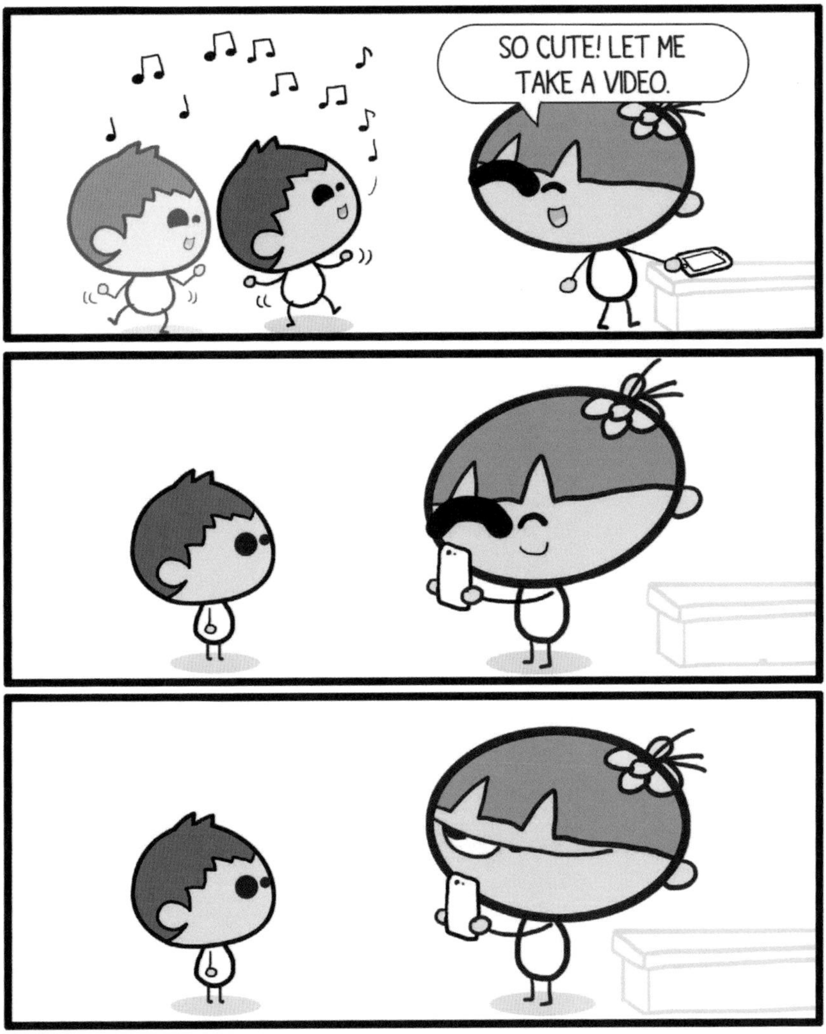
SO CUTE! LET ME TAKE A VIDEO.

THERE IS ALWAYS A WAY TO BREAK THE RULES

MAMA SPILLED SOMETHING AGAIN. DON'T STEP ON IT THIS TIME!!!
CAN'T SIT ON IT EITHER!!
WIGGLE WIGGLE

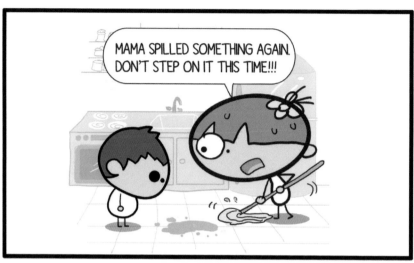

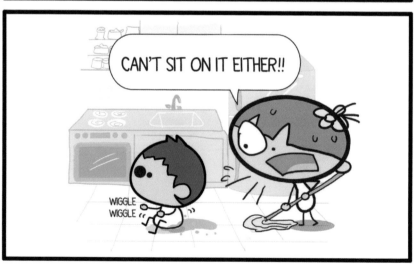

NIGHT AND DAY

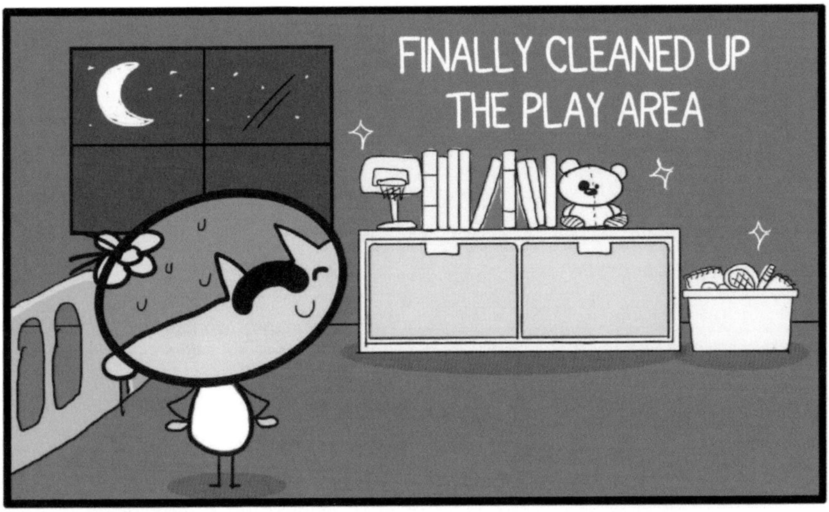
FINALLY CLEANED UP THE PLAY AREA

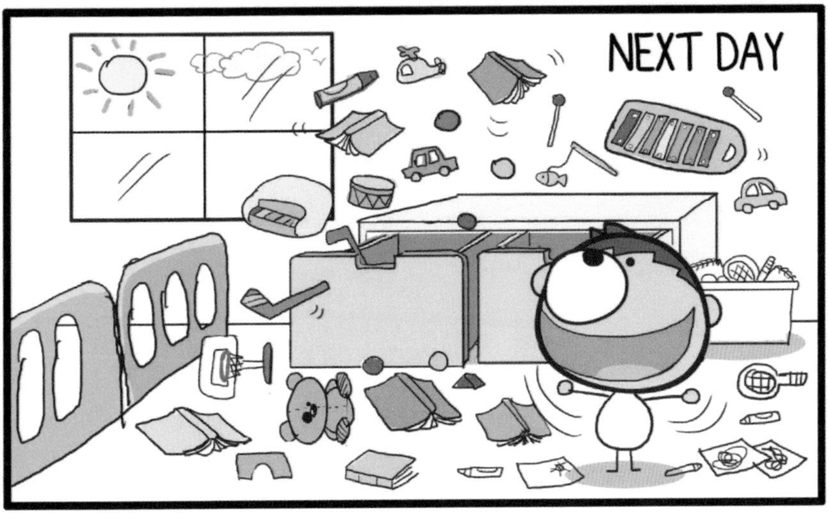
NEXT DAY

JUST SLEEP

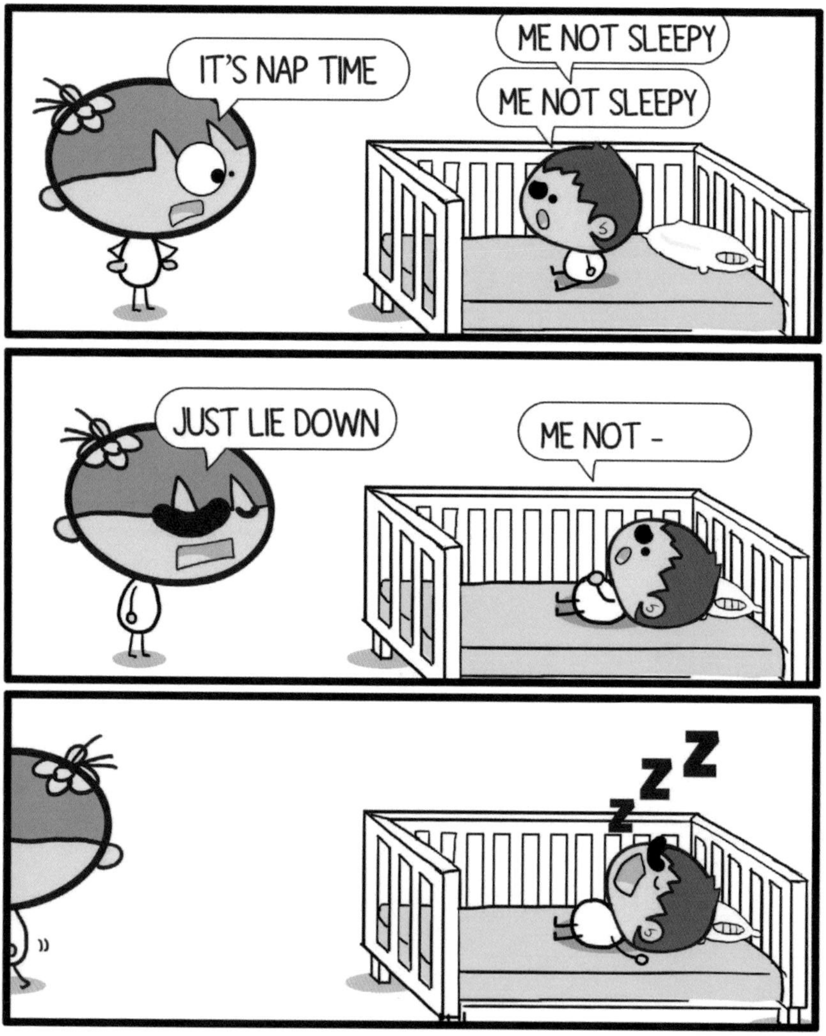
IT'S NAP TIME
ME NOT SLEEPY
ME NOT SLEEPY
JUST LIE DOWN
ME NOT -
Z
Z
Z

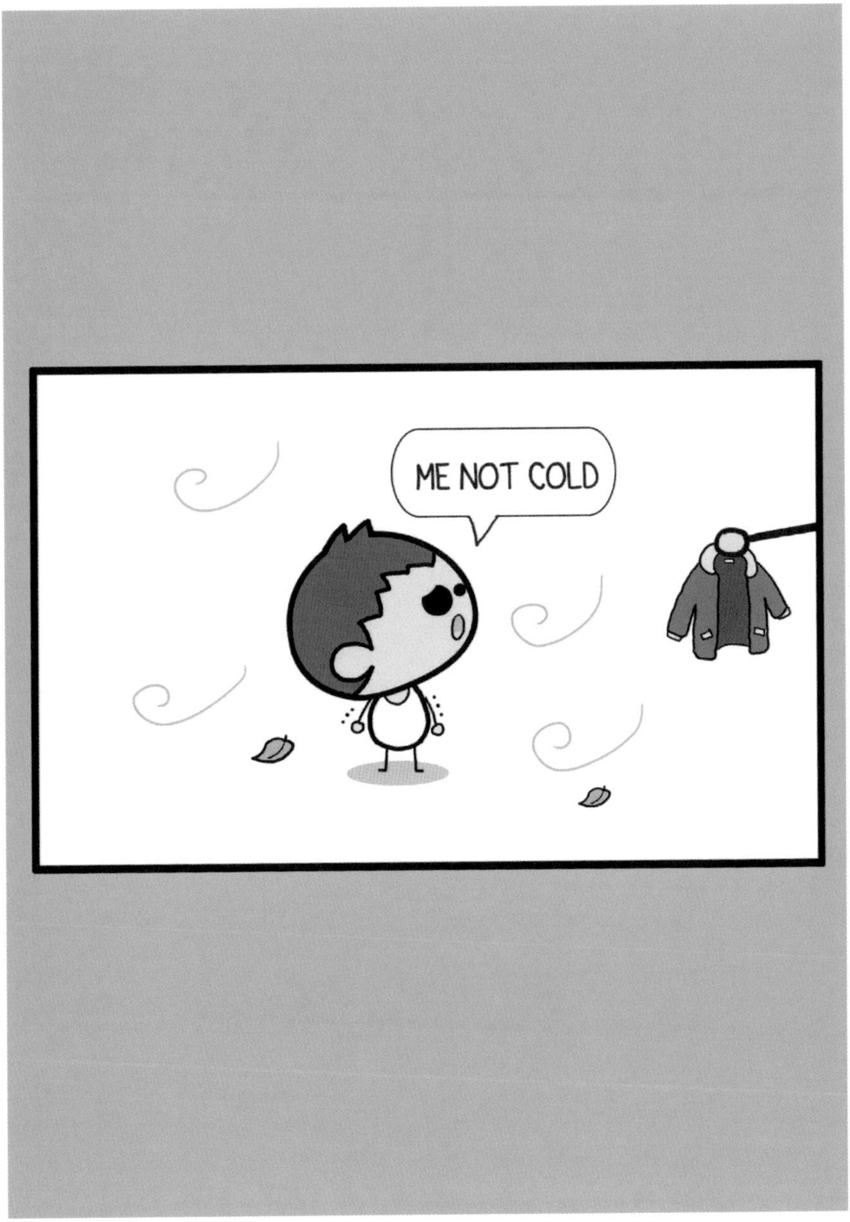
ME NOT COLD

BEDTIME

WHAT TIME DOES YOUR SON GO TO BED?
HE GOES TO BED AT 8PM
~WOW
THEN ASKS FOR WATER AT 8:15, SINGS AT 8:45, ASKS TO PEE AT 9, PEES AGAIN AT 9:15, ASKS TO WATCH TV AT 10, ROLLS AROUND FOR 2 HOURS, FALLS ASLEEP AT MIDNIGHT.

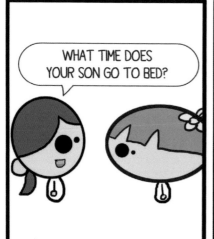

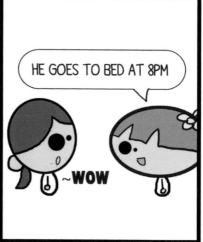

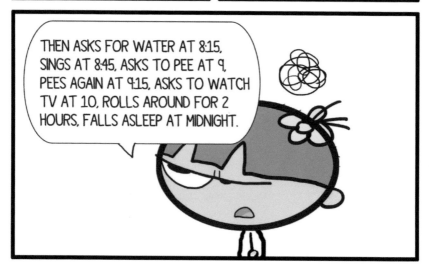

DECORATING THE CHRISTMAS TREE

AND FINALLY, WHERE DOES THE STAR GO?

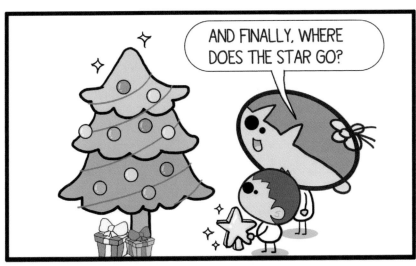

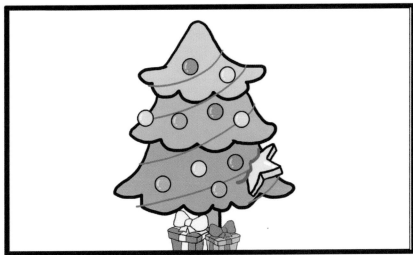

STAY SIMPLE SWEETIE, STAY SIMPLE

WOW!
WHAT?
TRUCK!
PLEASE DON'T GROW UP SO FAST.
WOW, BUS

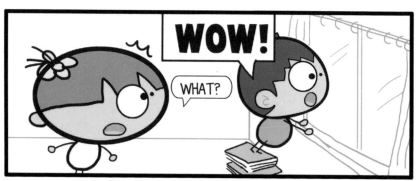

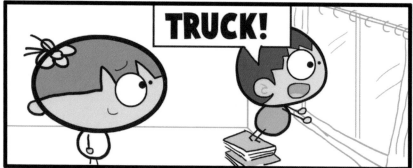

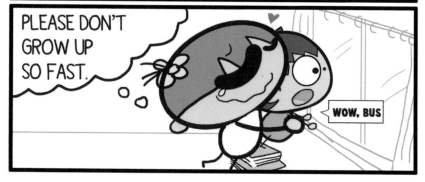

I WILL NEVER WIN, OR PEE PRIVATELY EVER AGAIN

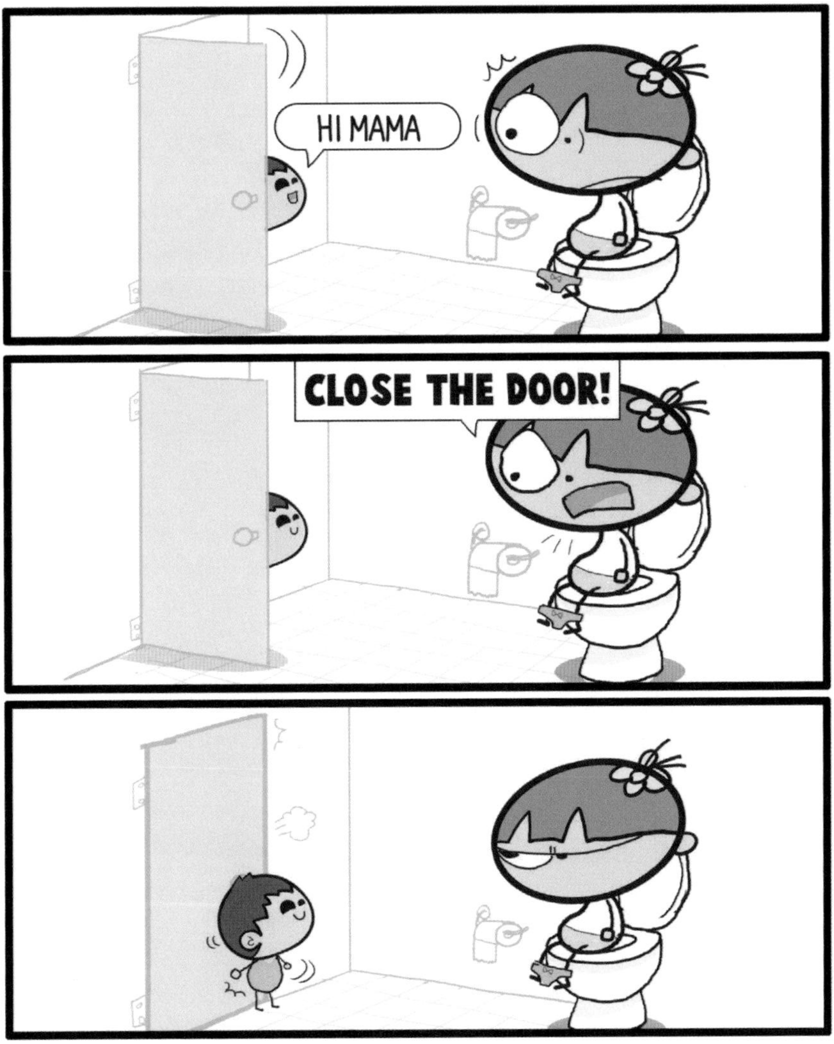
HI MAMA
CLOSE THE DOOR!

THE END

SUMMERANDMUU.COM

 @SummerAndMuu  fb.com/summerandmuucomics

 Brenda Li is a cartoonist and a motion graphic designer. At a young age, she moved from Hong Kong to Canada. She later graduated from The University of British Columbia studying Economics. Soon after, she realized she is not a money person, so she started learning graphics, animation and visual effects on her own. Known for her Summer and Muu comics, she was featured on Huffington Post, TV, radio and magazines. She was also a Visual Effects Artist for Transformers 3, Thor and Tron: Legacy.

Hope you enjoyed this book! If you are not chasing down a screaming kid at the moment and actually have time to spare, please leave me a review on the site ★ ★ ★ ★ ★ where you purchased this book! Thank you! ★ ★ ★ ★ ★

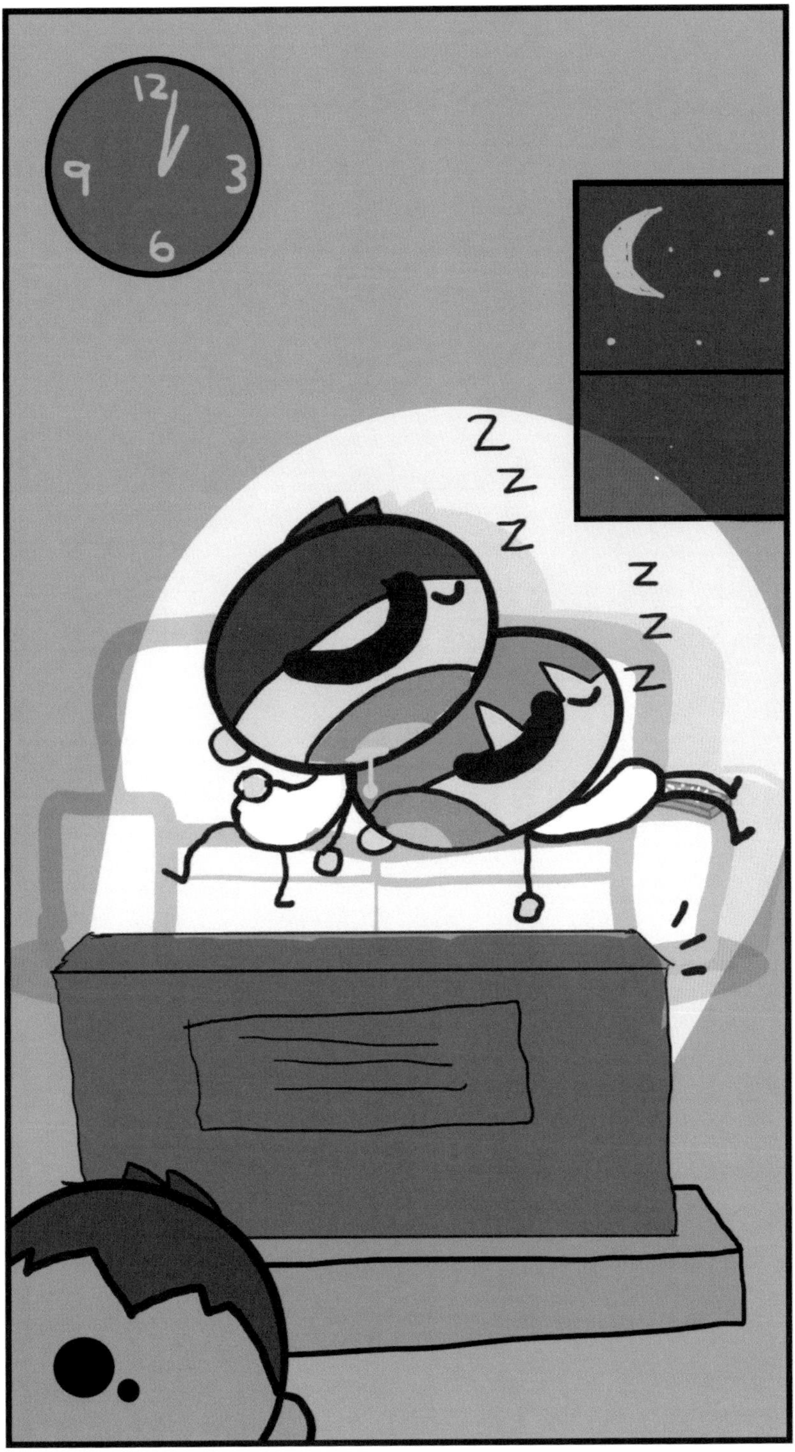
12
3
6
9
Z Z Z
Z Z Z

GOOD LUCK!

Printed in Great Britain
by Amazon